**The
Schreber
Case**

The
Schreber
Case

Psychoanalytic Profile
of a Paranoid Personality

by William G. Niederland, M.D.

Quadrangle/The New York Times Book Co.

Library of Congress Catalog Card Number: 73-79923

International Standard Book Number: 0-8129-0420-6

Design: Emily Harste

To
JACKIE
and my sons
JAMES
DANIEL
ALAN

Contents

List of Illustrations

Acknowledgments

First of all, I wish to thank my wife, Jacqueline, for her constant encouragement, valuable counsel, and active as well as tireless cooperation, as editor, in preparing this book.

Several other persons have been helpful, among whom I mention Drs. Jacob A. Arlow, Robert C. Bak, and Norman Reider. I also am indebted to Mary J. Crowther and Lucy Freeman for their interest and helpful advice.

I wish to thank a number of authors and publishers for permission to reprint various papers, or excerpts thereof, in particular Drs. Arthur C. Carr, Maurits Katan, and Robert B. White. Their articles appeared originally in: *The Psychoanalytic Quarterly, The International Journal of Psycho-Analysis, The Psychoanalytic Study of the Child*, and the *Journal of the American Psychoanalytic Association*.

Introduction

To this day, Freud's most important contribution to the psychoanalytic exploration of psychotic illness is his penetrating study of the Schreber case.

No adequate appraisal of Freud's work is possible unless one considers that in the opening years of our century psychology and psychiatry, in their approach to the nature, origin, and treatment of mental illness, had reached an impasse. In 1906 Paul Möbius, professor of psychiatry at the University of Heidelberg, had written a book entitled *The Hopelessness of All Psychology*. Occasional efforts to enter what was then thought to be the private life of a human being—that is, his innermost feelings and fantasies—were dismissed as "toying with thoughts." Apart from psychological speculations, at times intuitive and searching, no scientific attempt had been made to explore in depth the verbal outpourings of mentally ill people, let alone the written self-revelations of a psychotic patient who had recorded his apparently incomprehensible experiences, persecutory fears, and tormenting delusions in an extraordinary autobiographical memoir.

"Word salad" (plain or copious gibberish) was a favorite term used to designate, indeed dismiss, what appeared to be a mixture of rambling speech, unintelligible and loquacious talk, grotesque accusations, and alliterative nonsense so often employed by such patients. Most pre-Freudian psychiatrists and psychologists found all this fatiguing, and the patient who persisted in his verbal outpourings and bizarre mannerisms soon became a bore.

Then, in 1911, Freud published his famous "Psycho-Analytic Notes upon an Autobiographical Account of a Case of Paranoia," derived from his study of the autobiography mentioned above. In this work he analyzed the patient's mental productions, which he recognized as a complex network of ideas, memories, fantasies, sensations, conflicts, complaints, unfulfilled wishes, actual or fantasied experiences, the unraveling of which brought to light the connective lines between the past and present, the individual's personal history and his current psychological state (or illness). Indeed, expert unraveling and interpreting enabled Freud to understand, and to make others understand, the deeper meaning of those seemingly incoherent ramblings, irrational modes of expression, and other manifestations of seriously disturbed mental patients.

One such patient was Daniel Paul Schreber (1842–1911). He had been a distinguished jurist in the erstwhile kingdom of Saxony and in 1893 had been promoted to the high office of *Senatspräsident* in Dresden, that is, president of the kingdom's Superior Court of Appeals. Shortly after his assumption of the presidency, Schreber fell ill with a mental disease diagnosed as paranoia, which caused his confinement in a mental institution for almost nine years. During the last years of his hospital stay, in 1900 or so, Schreber, who had been making copious notes on his mental and physical state during the early years of his disease, began to write a book on his illness and the many strange inner experiences he suffered with it—that is, a book on the condition which had necessitated his hospitalization from 1893 to 1902. After his discharge from the hospital, Schreber published his book. It appeared in Leipzig (Saxony), in 1903, under the title *Denkwürdigkeiten eines Nerven-kranken* (Memoirs of a Mental Patient), hereinafter referred to as the *Memoirs*.

In this extraordinary book, the man who had been the presiding judge of the Saxonian Superior Court described in great detail not only his life in various mental institutions—indeed, during his many years of confinement he had been in three such places, all in Saxony—but also his tortured psyche before and during his illness. It is a frank, albeit garbled, story of a para-noiac's troubled mind, including the multiple symptoms, distressing delusions, fearful sensations, and other afflictions by which he was tortured. Schreber's original account was so frank that certain passages and one whole chapter of his manuscript were deleted as "unfit" for publication even before the book could appear in print; so frank, moreover, that many copies of the book were bought up and destroyed by the Schreber family after its publication. The few copies of the original *Memoirs* that remained attracted, of course, wide attention in psychiatric circles. One of these copies came into Freud's possession in Vienna in 1910 through the efforts of a Dresden physician, Dr. Stegmann, who also communicated to Freud the patient's age at the outbreak of the second illness: 51 years.

In the *Memoirs* Schreber also disclosed that in 1884–85—that is, nine years before the outbreak of his second (and lasting) disease—he had suf-fered from a mental disorder then called *hypochondriasis*, which had in-capacitated him for several months. He recovered from this first illness in a relatively short time and in his book he referred to it only in passing.

In reading Schreber's involuted, redundant, and often grotesque account, Freud soon found that it offered much that was interesting and illuminating. He later called it an "invaluable book" (1923). Freud refers to his work on the *Memoirs* in some of his 1910 correspondence. In a letter to Karl Abraham, dated December 16, 1910, for example, he writes: ". . . my own work, just finished, is on Schreber's book and tries to solve the riddle of paranoia. . . ."

From the time of its appearance in 1911 and continuing up to the present, Freud's analytic study of the *Memoirs* has aroused admiration and consensus on the one hand, and disapprobation and controversy on the other. The most frequent objection has been that in analyzing Schreber's psychosis, Freud wrote about a patient he had never seen. In anticipation of just such criticism, Freud made it clear that in working on Schreber's *Memoirs* he had applied his previous clinical experiences with paranoid individuals and, in addition, had found in Schreber's autobiographical account those very data which could well take the place of direct and personal contact with the patient.

Freud's Schreber analysis was a seminal event. It became the forerunner of numerous related studies in the broad area of paranoid conditions. The professional and nonprofessional literature on the subject is voluminous indeed. It is significant, therefore, that Freud repeatedly emphasized that he had used "a policy of restraint" in his work on the *Memoirs* and had limited himself exclusively to their interpretation, with the exception of one single fact: the patient's age when he fell ill for the second time. Freud also recognized that with the publication of his monograph, the investigation of the Schreber case was far from over. He suggested that analysts should trace countless details of the case history to their specific sources. He himself later added further comments to his Schreber analysis: a postscript, in 1912; in his paper "On Narcissism," in 1914; in his discussion of "A Neurosis of Demoniacal Possession in the Seventeenth Century," in 1923; and in the monograph "The Ego and the Id," in 1927.[1]

The studies by Freud on paranoia as such predate as well as postdate his Schreber analysis by many years. They go back to January, 1895, when he sent a lengthy note on the topic to his friend Wilhelm Fliess, and continue virtually to the end of his life in 1939, when he wrote his essays "Constructions in Analysis" and "An Outline of Psychoanalysis."

A number of psychoanalysts, psychiatrists, and psychologists have subsequently contributed to the literature on the Schreber case. I shall refer to these writings in the present volume; some, whole or excerpted, are included in Part III.

My own research on the Schreber case began in 1951 with the publication of the first of several papers on the famous patient. This work proceeded through 1971–72, when I served as moderator of a panel on the Schreber case at the annual convention of the American Psychiatric Association in Washington, D.C.

The material is derived from my study of the following sources:

1. Schreber's *Memoirs* in the original German (Leipzig, 1903) and some of his unpublished, personal writings (letters and poems) in my possession
2. Numerous books, papers, and pamphlets of Schreber's father, Daniel Gottlieb Moritz Schreber, in the original German, published between 1839 and 1883, as well as an unpublished letter of one of Schreber, Jr.'s sisters
3. Biographical writings in the original German on Schreber's father, beginning with L. M. Politzer (1861) and E. Mangner (1876) up to A. Ritter (1936) and contemporary authors

---

[1] The original version, *Das Ich und das Es*, appeared in 1923.

4. Correspondence and personal interviews with a surviving member of the Schreber family in Germany[2]
5. Correspondence with Dr. K. Schilling (Verden, West Germany) and F. von Lepel (Berlin) erstwhile president and member, respectively, of some local chapters of the German Schreber associations (*Schreber Vereine*)
6. Freud's Schreber analysis (1911)
7. Various scientific papers and an autobiographical fragment by Dr. Paul Theodor Flechsig, the psychiatrist of Schreber, during the latter's first illness and the early months of his second illness
8. Correspondence and personal interviews with Dr. F. Baumeyer who, between 1946 and 1949, was psychiatrist-in-charge of a hospital near Dresden (Saxony) and found the medical case records of Schreber's confinements in a mental institution (Sonnenstein sanatorium)
9. Methodical personal research in archives in Germany and elsewhere, on the basis of which the genealogical tables of the Schreber family and other authentic data pertaining to the case history were developed.

All the above material, collected during the course of my investigation and supplemented by further research, has enabled me to gain access to and reconstruct essential facts of Schreber's early life and development. It has also thrown light on numerous details and obscurities in Schreber's case history. And finally, of utmost importance, it has made it possible to correlate the bizarre mental formations in Schreber's delusional system (including florid fantasies, distorted images, hallucinatory experiences) to specific events in the early father-son relationship and thus to demonstrate the nucleus of truth in the son's paranoid productions.

Mentally ill people have always been "aliens" to fellow men not thus afflicted. The autobiography of Daniel Paul Schreber, a full-scale psychiatric exposé written by the patient himself and therefore not subject to the restrictions observed by physicians in accordance with medical ethics, will help the reader to view the considerable abnormality of such a man as less foreign and his personality as more human.

Through many centuries, and during the Dark Ages in particular, mental patients were thought to be possessed by the Devil or evil spirits. The prevailing cure consisted in expelling the Devil through exorcism or related efforts. Schreber's explicit ideas about *soul murder, soul voluptuousness,* and the *ceaseless influx of rays* into his body (see pp. 16–20) suggest the presence of similar notions in the patient. As our brief survey of the history of paranoia (Chapter 5) indicates, the emergence of exorcistic tendencies and procedures points to a revival of this type of thinking in our time.

[2] I wish to express my gratitude to Mrs. F. H. (Germany) for her helpful cooperation.

PART I

BACKGROUND

1 / Who Was
Daniel Paul Schreber?

The man who was to become "the most frequently quoted patient" (76) in modern psychiatry, was born in Leipzig, Germany, on July 25, 1842. On both his father's and his mother's side, he was the descendant of illustrious families, members of which had distinguished themselves in academic, cultural, and social activities of various kinds, especially in science and medicine.

Two of Schreber's paternal ancestors, Daniel Gottfried Schreber (1708–1777) and his son (the patient's great-uncle) Johann Christian Daniel von Schreber (1739–1810), knighted for his scientific achievements, held important positions at German universities and made notable contributions to biology, zoology,[1] botany, agriculture, history, and other fields of knowledge.

The following genealogical table lists some of his maternal and paternal forebears. The patient was extremely proud of his ancestry and references to it appear, often camouflaged or delusionally distorted, in various sections of the *Memoirs*.

From this table, the reader can readily see that Schreber's pride in his lineage was well-founded. However, the megalomanic elaboration of this fierce pride during his illness led him into such grandiose fabrications as transforming the name of his paternal grandmother into Frederick the Great (in German, *Friedrich der Grosse*), or thinking of himself as the descendant of the imaginary "Margraves of Tuscany and Tasmania."

The greatest impact on the son was made by his charismatic father, Dr. Daniel Gottlieb Moritz Schreber, whose influence persists in Germany and German-speaking parts of central Europe up to the present. In fact, every German knows the word *Schrebergarten* (Schreber garden) and many use the verb *schrebern* as a synonym for gardening. Very few, however, connect these terms with the name of the man who created the *Schreber movement* and whose teachings inspired the development of the Schreber gardens as well as the *Schreber Vereine*, associations devoted to the methodical cultivation of activities in fresh air, gymnastics, gardening, calisthenics, and sport.

Some excerpts from an article in the *New Yorker*, of September 19, 1959,

---

[1] On display in the Museum of Natural History (New York) is a specimen of *canis lycaon Schreberi*, the gray Eastern timber wolf, classified and described by Johann Christian Daniel von Schreber.

3

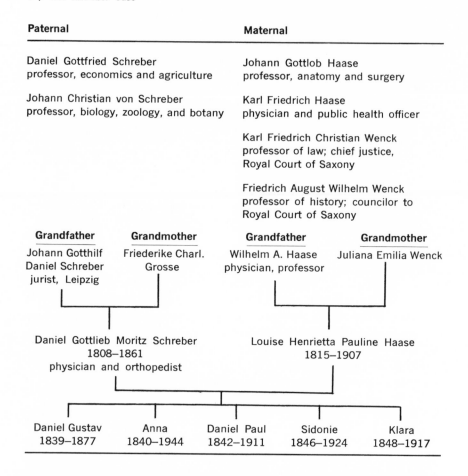

Paternal		Maternal	
Daniel Gottfried Schreber professor, economics and agriculture		Johann Gottlob Haase professor, anatomy and surgery	
Johann Christian von Schreber professor, biology, zoology, and botany		Karl Friedrich Haase physician and public health officer	
		Karl Friedrich Christian Wenck professor of law; chief justice, Royal Court of Saxony	
		Friedrich August Wilhelm Wenck professor of history; councilor to Royal Court of Saxony	

Grandfather	**Grandmother**	**Grandfather**	**Grandmother**
Johann Gotthilf Daniel Schreber jurist, Leipzig	Friederike Charl. Grosse	Wilhelm A. Haase physician, professor	Juliana Emilia Wenck

Daniel Gottlieb Moritz Schreber
1808–1861
physician and orthopedist

Louise Henrietta Pauline Haase
1815–1907

Daniel Gustav 1839–1877	Anna 1840–1944	Daniel Paul 1842–1911	Sidonie 1846–1924	Klara 1848–1917

and one in *The New York Times,* of June 2, 1960, may illustrate for the American reader the meaning and significance of the Schreber gardens in today's Germany.

The *New Yorker* article deals with a report from West Berlin and states:

It would not be exaggerating much to say that the dearest wish of just about every West Berliner is to have a *Schrebergarten,* or allotment garden—a patch of land (also known as a *Kleingarten,* or small garden, and with reason, since in many instances it measures only five square yards or so), where he would gladly devote an implausible amount of time and loving care to the raising of a few flowers or vegetables. . . .

. . . I came upon a large cluster of *Kleingärten* laid out on a site in Britz, a working-class district. Some people were tending their little plots with laborious care—weeding, pruning, cultivating, watering. Others had called it a day and were sitting in tiny arbors beside their gardens, enjoying a glass of beer. An air of almost rural peace pervaded the place, which, I discovered when I wandered on, was only a ten-minute walk from the East German boundary. . . .

The New York Times' article, dateline Bonn, reports:

When the *Schrebergärten* start to bloom in West Germany, everyone knows that summer is at hand.

Literally "allotment garden," the *Schrebergarten* amounts to a kind of people's agriculture in Germany. The small rented plots of land, rarely exceeding a few hundred square feet, are tilled with great preoccupation by many able-bodied men, women, and children in urban areas.

There is hardly a plot of land in German cities, no matter how miserable, that is not being avidly cultivated by amateur gardeners. *Schrebergärten* fill every empty lot, crowd against railway embankments, and advance inexorably up to factory walls.

Despite the chill weather that has settled over much of Germany in the last few days, the ubiquitous *Schrebergärten* are covered with a fresh green carpet of potato plants, cabbages, carrots, beans, and a splended proliferation of flowers.

Some of these gardens are elaborate affairs with tool sheds fashioned like Chinese pagodas, spurting fountains, and wide leafy bowers. Others are poor, rocky plots containing a few cabbage leaves.

It should be noted that the authors of both articles were unaware, as is the average German, of the real meaning and derivation of the word *Schrebergarten*. In both cases, it was translated, for lack of a better term, into "allotment garden."

Freud, however, was well aware of Dr. Schreber's reputation and fame. He wrote (1911): "the father of *Senatspräsident* Schreber was no insignificant person. He was the Dr. Daniel Gottlieb Moritz Schreber whose memory is kept green to this day by the numerous Schreber Associations. . . ."

As early as 1861, the physician L. Politzer, on the occasion of Dr. Schreber's death, spoke of him as a giant to be ranked among those rare individuals who through sheer force of personality are capable of effecting change in the attitudes of their contemporaries. In his life no less than in his work, Politzer said, Dr. Schreber was the embodiment of the audacious reformer, determined to follow the course of his own teachings and imagination. Politzer's glowing eulogy closed on this note: if every century and every country were to produce men of Dr. Schreber's stature, mankind and its future would be out of danger.

There was of course more to this interesting man. My research has brought to light additional qualities and activities that, though not always lacking in the personality of a zealous reformer, give Dr. Schreber the character of uniqueness. These elements will be described in detail in those sections of the present volume which deal with Schreber's father.

Suffice it to say at this point that Dr. Schreber's lifelong and enthusiastic pursuits for the promotion of physical health stemmed from his having been a sickly child, undersized and in frail health. Even in his college years he is described as having been *"von dürftiger Gestalt"* (of very poor physique) and possibly having suffered from pulmonary tuberculosis in adolescence.

Because of these conditions and his small size—he was probably not more than three-quarters of an inch over five feet tall—Dr. Schreber seems to have been exempt from military service. Through systematic bodily exercise and relentlessly pursued calisthenics he developed into a "strong and robust man, excellent gymnast, and outstanding swimmer and horseman." (77)

During the course of his professional career, Dr. Schreber constructed a whole system of physical exercise, which he called "medical indoor gymnastics." His theories for proper body care and growth received wide circulation through the publication of his numerous books, which were translated into many languages, including English. He expounded these theories in his lectures, by which he further spread the good-health "gospel." He applied these same ideas in the upbringing of his two sons.

His second son was the patient, Daniel Paul Schreber. The following tables will serve to outline the family constellation as well as the chronology of the patient's life.

Early Family Constellation

Father: Daniel Gottlieb Moritz Schreber
Mother: Pauline, née Haase

  Brother: Gustav, unmarried, committed suicide
  Sister: Anna, married
  Patient: *Daniel Paul,* married (one year after brother's suicide)
  Sister: Sidonie, unmarried
  Sister: Klara, married

Chronology of the Patient's Life and Illnesses

1842, July 25	Born in Leipzig.
1858 or 1859	Father suffers an accident with cerebral involvement and consequences.
1861, November	Father, age 53, dies of intestinal obstruction in a Leipzig hospital.
1877	Brother (three years his senior) commits suicide, age 38.
1878	Marries Sabine, née Behr, 15 years his junior. Subsequently, wife has several spontaneous abortions or miscarriages, probably six in all.
1884, October	Defeated as candidate for election to the *Reichstag.* A local newspaper carried this mocking headline: "Who, After All, Knows Dr. Schreber?"
1884, November	Consults with Dr. Paul Theodor Flechsig, chairman of the department of psychiatry, University Hospital, Leipzig. At this time, Schreber was chief judge of a provincial court in Chemnitz.
1884, December 8 through 1885, May 31	Stays in psychiatric hospital, Leipzig (Dr. Flechsig's *Nervenklinik);* makes two suicidal attempts in the hospital.

1885, June	Discharged from hospital, apparently recovered.
1886, January through 1893, September	*Landesgerichtsdirektor*, that is, presiding judge of an inferior court in Leipzig, a transfer from the same post held in Chemnitz (Saxony).
1893, October	Promoted to presiding judge, Court of Appeals, in Dresden, capital of Saxony.
1893, November 9 or 10	Consults with Dr. Flechsig in Leipzig; attempts suicide during the night of November 9 or 10 in his mother's home in Leipzig.
1893, November 21 through 1894, June 14	Readmitted to psychiatric hospital in Leipzig.
1894, June 14–28	Stays briefly in Lindenhof sanatorium, headed by Dr. Pierson.
1894, June 29 through	Confined to Sonnenstein sanatorium, in Pirna (near Dresden).
1902, December 20	Discharged from Sonnenstein sanatorium; returns to wife and home.
1903	The *Memoirs* published.
	(Though his recovery was only partial, Schreber remained in relatively fair mental health for several years, and was able to function as a lawyer, though in limited fashion, writing occasional legal briefs and the like. Nonetheless, one serious vestige of his illness remained: his conviction that he was a woman with female breasts and other feminine attributes.)
1907, May	Mother dies, age 92.
1907, November 14	Wife suffers a stroke; dies May, 1912.
1907, November 27 through	Readmitted to a mental hospital in Leipzig-Dösen.
1911, April 14	Dies, age 68, in Leipzig-Dösen.

The chronology shows that during his lifetime, Schreber experienced three serious mental breakdowns that necessitated hospitalization. Diagnostically speaking, these illnesses were manifestations of the same disease: in today's terminology, paranoid schizophrenia.

Summing up, the three breakdowns occurred in:

1884–85: six months' duration; illness then diagnosed as severe hypochondriasis
1893–1902: nine years' duration; illness then diagnosed as paranoia (*Dementia paranoides*)
1907–11: four years' duration; illness then diagnosed as paranoia.

Altogether, Daniel Paul Schreber spent close to 14 years of his life in mental institutions. At the height of his career he had attained one of the most prestigious legal positions in the erstwhile kingdom of Saxony.

In 1911, the very year of Schreber's death, Freud published his classic monograph "Psycho-Analytic Notes upon an Autobiographical Account of a Case of Paranoia (Dementia Paranoides)," which unknown to the patient was to immortalize him in the world of analytic and psychiatric literature.

2 / Excerpts from the Memoirs

Freud called Schreber's *Memoirs* an invaluable book. This it is, and a difficult book too. It is the autobiography of a psychiatric patient with superior intellectual endowment, or, more precisely, a description of the emotional and physical states in which he found himself during the years of his confinement in mental institutions.

During the early period of his (second) illness he was highly agitated, suicidal, regressive, and disorganized to a degree that made any systematized activity such as writing a full and coherent account of his condition well nigh impossible. The hospital records indicate, for example, that after a visit from his wife he asked the attendant whether she had been a live person and, if so, whether she had stepped out of her grave. At other times he felt that he was dead and rotten, bellowed at the sun, which he called a whore, frequently requested "the potassium cyanide destined for me," accused the doctors and nurses of plotting against him, spoke with God, and had many other terrifying visual and auditory hallucinations. He also tried to drown himself in the bathtub and many times refused to take food.

Even during this period of almost total confusion and mental disorganization Schreber made notes on scraps of paper. This was later followed by diary entries and more detailed annotations, "initially without any thought of publishing them." In 1900, when the more acute phase of his psychosis had subsided and he undertook legal steps for his release from the mental institution and tutelage[1]—steps that ultimately led to his discharge from the Sonnenstein sanatorium, he began to consider that it might be his service "to science and the promotion of religious truths" to report on his observations concerning his body, personal experiences, and God's universe.

I leave it to philosophers and theologians to determine whether the *Memoirs*, with their innumerable references to God, universe, religion, the hereafter, are of interest to their respective fields of thought and endeavor. As a psychoanalyst and psychiatrist I can unequivocally state that their clinical value is as unquestionable today as it was at the time of their ap-

[1] Legal action in the German juridical system aimed at the restoration of the competence of a patient who had been declared insane and had therefore been placed under guardianship by the courts.

pearance in print in 1903 and their analysis by Freud in 1911. The exceptional achievement was twofold: on the part of the patient, who, suffering from one of the most devastating types of mental disease, succeeded in transmitting to posterity a full account of his psychosis, including its massive pathology and florid symptomatology; on the part of Freud, who succeeded in unraveling the relevant dynamics from what had seemed a hopeless tangle of incomprehensible verbiage or, at best, a fantastic set of extravagant imagery.

Schreber's book was translated into English by I. Macalpine and R. A. Hunter (76) in 1955. Their work has merit, especially in view of the difficulties presented by Schreber's involuted sentences, frequent neologisms, and many peculiarities of language, style, and form. In various sections of his book, he used a special terminology, which he called *"Grundsprache"* (ground language or root language) and which he attributed to God or divine *rays.* In his text, this type of language is interwoven with personal, political, and religious beliefs, philosophical speculations, and hallucinatory experiences.

His delusional system, as it is revealed in the *Memoirs,* can be summarized briefly as follows:

He felt he had a mission to redeem the world and to restore it to its lost state of bliss.

This mission must be preceded by the destruction of the world and by his personal transformation into a woman.

Transformed into a female, he—Schreber, now a woman—would become God's mate, and out of such union a better and healthier race of men would emerge.

I believe the reader should have an opportunity to study some of the original content of the *Memoirs.* He will thus be able to form a first-hand impression of the texture and complexity of Schreber's productions. The first chapter which deals with God and immortality opens in this way:

The human soul is located in the nerves of his body the physical nature of which is such that as a layman I cannot state more than that they are structures of extraordinary delicacy—like the finest thread—and that man's entire spiritual life rests on their excitability by external stimuli. They produce vibrations in the nerves which give rise to a feeling of pleasure and unpleasure in an unexplainable way; they have the capacity of retaining the recollection of the impressions received by them (the human memory); they also have the capacity to cause the muscles of the body which they inhabit to move. . . . From the most delicate beginnings (as the human fruit of the body, as the soul of the child) they develop into a multi-layered system that encompasses the most extensive areas of human knowledge (the soul of a mature human being). . . . Part of the nerves is only capable of receiving sensory stimuli (visual, auditory, taste, voluptuous nerves, etc.) . . . other nerves (the nerves of reason) receive and preserve mental impressions and as the organs of will power give to the whole organism of man the impulse to express his ability to respond forcefully to the influences of the external world. . . . Each nerve of reason represents the entire spiritual individuality of man, as though the totality of memories were imprinted in every single nerve of reason. . . .

God is a priori solely nerve, not body, and therefore akin to the human soul. God's nerves, however, are infinite and eternal unlike those in the human body in which they exist only in a limited number. They have the same properties which human nerves possess, but to a degree of potency which transcends all of man's ideas. In particular, they are capable of converting themselves into all possible things of the created world; in this function they are named rays. . . .

In this same chapter there is further elaboration of God's attributes and actions as manifested by the heavenly bodies, the stars, and especially the sun which

has spoken with me in human words for years and for that reason can be recognized as a living being or as an organ of a superior being standing behind it. God also makes the weather . . . and the proud statement on the occasion of the destruction of the Spanish Armada of Philip II in 1588 *"Deus afflavit et dissipati sunt"* (God blew the wind and they were dispersed) most likely contains a historical truth.

Schreber continues: "the nerves of *living* human beings, especially in a state of great excitement, possess such power of attraction for God's nerves that God would have been unable to get away from them and thus his own existence would have been endangered."

In a lengthy footnote, Schreber adds that *"a force of attraction* emanating from individual bodies—and in my case—from one single human body over such enormous distances . . . may appear quite absurd. Nonetheless, the action of the force of attraction is a fact that for me is absolutely unquestionable. . . ."

He then proceeds:

A regular exchange between God and human souls occurred in the order of the Universe only after death. God could approach corpses without danger in order to draw out of the body up to Himself their nerves, in which self-consciousness[2] was not extinguished, but remained latent, by dint of the force of the rays and to awaken them to a new heavenly life; self-consciousness returned through the action of the rays. The new life in the hereafter is a *state of bliss* . . . for God—or if one prefers in Heaven—only pure human nerves were usable, because they were destined to become attached to God himself and finally to turn into parts of God as "forecourts of heaven," so to speak. . . .

The male state of bliss was on a higher level than the female state of bliss; the latter seems to have consisted of an uninterrupted sensation of constantly felt voluptuousness . . . it was the ultimate goal of all souls, merged with other

[2] Schreber uses the German term *Selbstbewusstsein*, which literally translated is "self-consciousness." However, in this context, the meaning is clearly *consciousness*.

souls, to coalesce into higher entities and to feel themselves as parts of God ("forecourts of heaven")....

Chapter I of the *Memoirs* concludes with a further description of God's nature which is divided by "a strange partition according to which a lower God (Ahriman) and an upper God (Ormuzd) were delineated." Schreber finds this division in various religions and notes that he learned about it from the voices that talked to him at the beginning of July, 1894, or thereabouts. To this description he adds that

omniscience and *omnipresence* of God did not exist in the sense that He constantly saw inside each human being, observed every feeling in the nerves, and tested "heart and kidneys" at every point of time . . . the whole order of the universe appears as a "miraculous structure"[3] the greatness of which transcends in my view all conceptions which men and nations have formed about their relation to God in the course of history.

In Chapter II of the *Memoirs,* the patient records that "in recent times a rent has occurred in this 'miraculous structure' which is closely related to my personal destiny." But to describe the deeper connections and "obscure processes which can be only partially unveiled on the basis of my personal experiences," is not possible, since

I must rely on guesswork and supposition. I wish to state from the outset that the earliest beginnings in the genesis of this development stretch far back, perhaps to the eighteenth century, in part to the important roles played by the names Flechsig and Schreber (presumably not limited to any individual member of these families), and in part to the role played by the concept of *"soul murder."*

To begin with the latter, the thought that it is possible to gain power in some way over the soul of another person in order to attain longer life at the expense of such a soul or to achieve some other advantages outlasting death, is widespread in the folkloric literature and poetry of all nations. I refer, for example, to Goethe's *Faust*, Lord Byron's *Manfred*, Weber's *Freischütz*, etc. . . . certainly the wide dissemination of the folkloric motif of "soul murder" or soul stealing gives food for thought because it is most unlikely that such concepts could have developed by so many peoples in virtually the same way without any factual basis. Since the voices which have talked to me from my first contacts with God (mid-March, 1894) have daily pointed to the fact of "soul murder" committed by someone as the cause of the crisis in the realms of God, and in earlier times Flechsig was named as the originator of the "soul murder," still more recently in deliberate reversal of the circumstances "soul murder" was attributed to me, I arrived at the assumption that at some point in the past a situation amounting to "soul murder" may have taken place between the Flechsig and Schreber families and that at the time when my nervous disease appeared to be incurable, "soul murder" on me, albeit without success, might have been attempted.

[3] In German: *Wundervoller Aufbau*, which is in the title of one of the most important books written by Schreber's father.

Probably after the first "soul murder," in accordance with the principle *l'appétit vient en mangeant*, further soul murders on the souls of other men followed . . . in this respect much remains obscure. Possibly, at first, a battle arising out of jealousy between souls which had already departed from life was involved. For both the Flechsigs and Schrebers belonged, as the expression had it, to "the highest heavenly nobility"; the Schrebers, in particular, had the title "Margraves of Tuscany and Tasmania," according to the habit of the souls to adorn themselves with somewhat arrogant earthly titles. Various names concerning both families come to mind, of the Flechsig family besides Professor Paul Theodor Flechsig a certain Abraham Fürchtegott Flechsig and a Daniel Flechsig who is said to have lived toward the end of the eighteenth century and to have been an "auxiliary devil" because of a soul murder-like situation. At any rate, for a long time I have been in nerve contact with Professor Paul Theodor Flechsig and Daniel Fürchtegott Flechsig . . . and have had parts of both their souls in my body. The soul of Daniel Fürchtegott Flechsig disappeared years ago (vanished altogether); of the soul of Professor Paul Theodor Flechsig, at least a part exists still today (i.e., a certain number of nerves which originally had the now considerably diminished identity awareness of Professor Paul Theodor Flechsig) as a "tested soul" in heaven. . . . What the essence of "soul-murder" really is, and so-to-speak the technique thereof, I cannot say aside from what was alluded to above. One might only add . . . [here Schreber's text is interrupted by a parenthesis containing the words: "The passage that follows is unfit for publication"].

Inasmuch as the present Professor Flechsig or one of his ancestors might be accused of being the originator of "soul murders," I am certain of at least one fact, that such a person must have some awareness of the supernatural things which I have meantime come to know, but he surely has not penetrated to a deeper knowledge of God and the order of the universe. . . .

This chapter, too, concludes with references to the power of attraction, the greatness and sublimeness of the deity, though "not even God is or was a being of such *absolute perfection* as most religions ascribe to Him"; references to God's further limitations including the fact that "the behavior of a single individual might endanger Him" who under certain circumstances "could even be seduced into a sort of conspiracy against human beings, however innocent"; and finally reference to "the passage of God's nerves into my body," a process so unwanted and uncomfortable that

every day I can hear the incessant cries for help in heaven coming from those parts of the nerves which have been separated from their total mass. But all these losses can be restored inasmuch as there is an *Eternity*, though perhaps thousands of years may be required for the full restitution of the previous state.

Chapter III of the *Memoirs* is missing. The text carries the following explanation:

The contents of Chapters I and II were necessary in preparation for what follows. What could thus far be described only in part as axiom, will now be clarified, if at all possible, in view of the circumstances.

I shall first deal with some occurrences involving other members of my family which might conceivably be related to the presupposed "soul murder," and which in any case are all of a more or less enigmatic nature, scarcely explainable in the light of common human experience.

Schreber's text ends abruptly at this point, and the following parenthetical statement is given: "(The further content of this Chapter is omitted from publication as unfit for print)." Despite all efforts by researchers—including the present author—this important section of the book has remained irretrievable. Presumably, this part of Schreber's original manuscript was destroyed by the publisher (and/or family ?) as early as 1903 or shortly thereafter.

Chapter IV opens with a chronological account of Schreber's first two illnesses. It will be recalled that he succumbed to his third mental illness only in 1907, four years after the publication of the *Memoirs*. He writes:

I now come to speak of *my own personal fortunes* during the periods when I suffered from two nervous diseases. Twice I have been ill with nerves, both times because of mental overwork, the first time (as chief judge of the Court in Chemnitz) on the occasion of my candidature for the *Reichstag*, the second time because of the unusual burden of work which I encountered on taking up the office of presiding judge of the Court of Appeals in Dresden to which I had been recently appointed.

The first illness began in the fall of 1884 and was totally cured by the end of 1885 so that I could resume my duties on January 1, 1886 as chief judge of the Court in Leipzig to which I had meantime been transferred. The second nervous illness began in October, 1893 and still persists. In both cases I spent the greater portion of the period of sickness in the clinic for mental diseases of the University of Leipzig chaired by Professor Dr. Flechsig, the first time from about mid-December 1884 to the beginning of June 1885, the second time from about mid-November 1893 until approximately mid-June 1894. In neither case, on entering the institution did I have the slightest idea that an antagonism existed between the Schreber and Flechsig families, nor did I know of any of the supernatural things with which I dealt in the foregoing chapters.

Schreber then mentions his gratitude to Dr. Flechsig and the even greater appreciation of his wife for the successful efforts of Dr. Flechsig in whom "she worshipfully saw the person who had restored her husband to her and whose picture she kept on her desk for years." The text continues:

After recovering from my first sickness, I lived with my wife for eight quite happy years, rich too in worldly honors and clouded only by the repeated unfulfilled hope for offspring. In June 1893 I received (first personally from the Minister of Justice Dr. Schurig) the notification of my impending promotion to the post of *Senatspräsident* [presiding judge] of the Court of Appeals in Dresden.

During this period I had several dreams to which I paid no special attention. ... I dreamt a number of times that my earlier nervous disease had returned, and just as I felt unhappy in the dream so did I feel fortunate on awakening that it had been only a dream. Furthermore, on one occasion while still lying in bed toward morning (whether half asleep or already awake, I do not know), I experienced a sensation which, on further thought in total wakefulness, struck me as most peculiar. It was the fantasy that it really must be quite lovely to be a woman submitting to sexual intercourse. This fantasy was so alien to my entire way of thinking that I can probably say that in full consciousness I would have rejected it with indignation; in view of what I have meanwhile experienced, however, I cannot entirely rule out the possibility that some external influences may have been operative in bringing about this fantasy.

On October 1, 1893 I assumed my new position as *Senatspräsident* of the Court of Appeals in Dresden. The burden of work I encountered as I mentioned before was extremely heavy. . . . The task was all the heavier and required all the more tact in my personal dealings inasmuch as the members of the (five-judge) panel over which I presided were for the most part older than I (by as much as 20 years), and were moreover better acquainted with the practices of the Court to which I had been only newly appointed. Thus it happened that after but a few weeks I became mentally overworked. Sleeping became difficult . . . and I began to take sodium bromide.

From then on certain disturbing noises at night "in the wall of our bedroom became noticeable . . . and having countless times thereafter heard similar noises," Schreber's initial suspicion concerning them soon led to his conviction that

right from the start a more or less defined plan must have existed to prevent my sleep and later my recovery from the disease which resulted from the insomnia. . . .

Thus my illness rapidly assumed a threatening character; already on the 8th or 9th day of November I was forced, upon the advice of Dr. O., to take a sick leave of eight days . . . in order to consult Dr. Flechsig in whom, from the time of his successful cure of the first sickness, we placed our full confidence. . . . [After a bad night in Chemnitz] (We, my wife and I) . . . travelled to the University Clinic to see Professor Flechsig who the day before by telegram had been prepared for our visit. A lengthy interview followed in the course of which Professor Flechsig developed a remarkable eloquence which did not fail to affect me.

Thereupon Schreber's mood improved somewhat and he spent the night at his mother's house in Leipzig. There he soon found himself in "a state of great excitement. . . . Sleeping drugs (camphor[4], etc.) . . . did not help." After spending the night in great anxiety and almost without sleep, Schreber made "preparations for a kind of suicide by means of a towel or the like," but was prevented from so doing by his wife. Professor Flechsig was called to the home the following morning, advised the patient's prompt admission to his psychiatric clinic and accompanied him personally to the hospital. There, the next days and nights were equally bad, the nights almost without sleep despite

[4] In the 1880s and 1890s, camphor was widely used as a sleep-producing drug in both Europe and America. It was also a standard remedy for what was then called melancholy.

the administration of somniforous remedies (camphor, etc.). The patient records: ". . . my mind was almost exclusively occupied with thoughts of death . . . the idea that there was no way left for a man for whom sleep could not be provided by any of the remedies of medical art, other than by taking his life, dominated me entirely." In fact, during one of those first nights at the hospital he made another suicide attempt by hanging.

Subsequently some improvement occurred, but from mid-February on a serious deterioration set in that continued through many months and years. Schreber records February 15, 1894 as the day "when my wife who until then had stayed with me every day for several hours and had regularly had lunch with me at the hospital, left on a four-day visit to her father in Berlin." With the wife absent,

important changes in my environment and myself occurred so that I could no longer see in her a live person but only a miracled-up human figure in the manner of the "fleetingly made men." Decisive for my mental breakdown was a particular night in the course of which I had a quite unusual number (perhaps half a dozen) of nocturnal emissions. At about that time also the first indications of contact with supernatural forces appeared . . . especially with Professor Flechsig who spoke with my nerves without being present in person. From this point on, I also gained the impression that Professor Flechsig was secretly plotting against me. . . .

In Chapters V through XII Schreber gives us a detailed report of the protean symptoms of his illness, with special reference to his ideas of persecution and massive hallucinations during his stay in psychiatric institutions. Many of these subjective experiences are explored at length with verbatim references to the *Memoirs* in the various studies included in the present volume. I point here to their analytic evaluation and interpretation as they appear farther along in the book.

Suffice it to say that it became evident to Schreber that a man in such circumstances as "in the case of world catastrophes which require the destruction of mankind . . . must be 'emasculated' [transformed into a female]." He felt himself "adversely influenced by certain persons," notably by the "soul murderer" Professor Flechsig and his attendants. The aim of Flechsig's plot was to gain control over the patient's soul and subject his body, transformed into that of a female, to gross "sexual abuse." There was even talk that his body would be "thrown to the hospital attendants for sexual misuse." In a revealing passage, he equates "soul murder" to castration and, thereby, to the destruction of his reason (Chapter V).

Schreber eventually developed the delusion that he actually was a woman, declaring that he had feminine breasts and experienced the "soul voluptuousness" of a female being. As for the end of the world, Schreber first thought that only a span of "two hundred years was allotted to the earth," but later felt that this period of time had already expired and that "I was the last real person left," whereas others, including Professor Flechsig, his attendants and patients, were nothing but "miracled-up, 'fleetingly made men.' " In this context he speaks of his innumerable visions of the destruction of the world which were "in part of a horrifying nature, but in part too of an indescribable splendor."

Ideas of grandeur and uniqueness are expressed frequently. One of these passages reads: ". . . since the creation of the world, there can hardly have been a case such as mine, in which a human being keeps continuous contact . . . not merely with *individual* departed souls but with the sum total of all souls and with God's omnipotence as well." On the other hand, foul masses were "unloaded into my body" and voices "accused me of masturbation."

Throughout most sections of the *Memoirs* an overwhelming number of divine miracles are recorded that, like numerous other events in the patient's hallucinatory world, are directed against his person. Some of these miracles were comparatively harmless—for example, the spectacle of the spontaneous generation of certain insects. But many of them were menacing and distressing indeed. (The genesis and nature of the so-called miracles are elucidated in Chapters 7, 8, 9 and 11 of the present volume.)

In Chapters XIII and XIV Schreber reports on a critical phase of his illness. Here again the month of November is a landmark for him. He writes:

An important time in the history of my life and my whole outlook on the possible development of my future was the month of November, 1895. . . . It was at this point that the signs of my bodily transformation into a woman became so strong that I could no longer escape the knowledge of the intrinsic goal at which the whole process was aimed. So close to completion was the miracle that during the nights just preceding this development, my penis might really have been retracted *in toto* [into the abdomen] if, in accordance with my sense of masculine honor, I had not fought against it with all my will. In any case, soul voluptuousness had become so intense that I myself accepted the configuration of a female body, first on my arms and hands, later on my legs, bosom, buttocks, and other body parts.

In the course of this development Schreber became more and more convinced that the order of the universe demanded his transformation into a woman. He saw himself confronted by two alternatives: "either to become an idiot in masculine shape and form, or a highly intelligent female." Thus, his choice of the latter course was a matter of mere "common sense."

To be sure, at first he was troubled by the admonitions on the part of certain rays that hypocritically appealed to his "sense of masculine honor." Many ordinary questions came to his mind such as, "Are you not ashamed in front of your wife?" Or more vulgar ones: for example, "Imagine a presiding judge who lets himself be fucked."[5] Simultaneously, a marked increase in sensuous pleasure occurred, a state of *"high-grade voluptuousness"* developed, and he decided to accept his new bodily condition without reserva-

---

[5] In the original, this word is printed f . . . . , from the German *ficken*.

tion. Schreber graphically records: "Since then I have fully inscribed the further cultivation of femininity on my banner and shall continue to do so . . . regardless of what others may think of me."

While these radical changes were taking place in Schreber's body, concomitant alterations occurred in the celestial spheres:

The merging with my body—due to the force of attraction—of those rays which were separated from the total mass of God's nerves, meant for the nerves involved the end of their independent existence, something akin to death in man. It was therefore only natural for God to set into motion all possible means by which He might escape the fate of perishing in my body along with those many parts separated from His total mass; one was not very discriminating about the means employed for this purpose. *The attraction, however, lost its terror for the nerves involved if and when they encountered a feeling of soul voluptuousness in my body*, in which they in turn participated. In my body they thus found a complete or almost complete substitute for the lost heavenly bliss which is equivalent to voluptuous pleasure.

Schreber explains that God's attitude toward him was likewise subject to change. At one time the upper God (Ormuzd) maintained a rather friendly relationship with Schreber, while the lower God (Ahriman) in alliance with Flechsig, plotted against him. At other times, the situation reversed and the lower God became friendly while the upper God manifested hostility.

Schreber also came to believe that God tended to withdraw from him if a state of soul voluptuousness was not maintained in his body. For this reason, Schreber says, soul voluptuousness and cultivation of femininity "serve the well understood interest of the rays, that is, of God Himself." But God could not learn from experience and "the incapacity to understand the living human person as an organism was common to both the lower and upper God." This inability puzzled Schreber and he arrived at the conclusion: *"Every attempt to educate outwards must be relinquished as hopeless."* Nor was Schreber able to persuade the remote God who periodically withdrew to great distances that he, Schreber, was not totally demented as God thought.

In the closing paragraphs of this section the author of the *Memoirs* offers a moving description of his tortured state of mind during this period in the hospital:

My sleep depends totally on the celestial constellations; as soon as God withdraws too far away . . . sleep becomes entirely impossible. If I then stay awake, the senseless rumbling of the voices in my head produces intolerable mental agony compounded on and off by fits of bellowing [mostly at the sun] which have lasted for more than a year. . . .

In this connection, he refers to "violent scenes" between other patients and himself, occasionally between him and the attendants as well. Outbursts of rage (*Tobsuchtsanfälle*) were frequent. For this reason apparently, he was locked up in a cell [padded cell?] containing nothing but an iron bedstead, a bedpan, and some bedding. In addition, most of the time the cell "was completely darkened by heavy wooden shutters." In concluding the chapter he reports that once in a state of rage during which he used his fists against the closed shutters, he knocked a shutter down. By "miracle it had already been loose and the cross-bar came down miraculously on my head with such force that my head and chest were covered with blood."[6]

In Chapters XV through XXI the patient broadens his discussion of the multiple phenomena he had described in the preceding sections of his book. Though he had begun to engage in various normal activities and to doubt some of his delusional ideas about "fleetingly made little men," the influence of rays, and so on, he still felt "alone with God . . . and as the only human being" in existence so far as God was concerned. People were only "lifeless shadows." But after observing a children's procession from his window he could no longer deny "that a real human race still did exist in the same number and local distribution as before." This presented difficulties for Schreber. He had to confess that he was confronted with "an unsolved mystery which might forever remain unsolved" because he could not understand the presence of these children in the light of his previous knowledge of the destruction of the world.

He also elaborates on his earlier observations regarding miracles. There were miraculously created birds that talked without understanding the meaning of their spoken words; constant miracles directed against his head, eyes, chest, abdomen, muscles, knee caps, coccyx bone, and other organs; miracles of being tied to celestial bodies; the bellowing miracle; the hot and cold miracles; the need to defecate, produced by miracle. On the latter function Schreber comments in some detail:

Like everything in my body, the need to defecate is caused by miracles . . .
this miracle belongs to the domain of the upper God and is repeated at least
several dozen times daily. It is linked to the idea of God's total lack of knowledge
of a living person as an organism, namely that "shitting"[7] is in a sense a final
thing, i.e., that the miracling-up of the urge to shit brings about the destruction
of reason and the possibility of a definite withdrawal of the rays. . . . As to the
symbolic meaning of the act of defecation, he who has developed a relationship
like mine to the divine rays may well be entitled to shit on the whole world.

In a later passage the patient adds his belief that God himself has a hand in the matter of evacuation.

Schreber then turns to the subject of "drawings" and "picturing" which he views as phenomena connected with the rays. He writes:

[6] The hospital records contain no indication of such an accident. While it may have occurred, it is more likely that the patient refers delusionally to the head injuries sustained by his father when he was struck by an iron bar in a gymnasium.

[7] In the original, this word is printed s . . . . . . n, from the German *scheissen*.

. . . lying in bed at night, I can create the impression for myself and the rays that my body is equipped with female breasts and female genitals. The drawing of female buttocks on my body—*honi soit qui mal y pense*—has become such a habit for me that I do it almost spontaneously each time I bend down.

Toward the end of his hospital stay the patient—now much calmer and more accessible to his doctors—records in the *Memoirs:*

For well over six years my body has been filled with these nerves of voluptuousness as a result of the ceaseless influx of rays or God's nerves. It is therefore understandable that my body is replete with nerves of voluptuousness to a degree unsurpassed by any female. . . . When [the rays] get closer, my chest gives the impression of a rather fully developed female bosom; this phenomenon can be *seen* by anyone who is willing to observe *me with his own eyes.* I am in a position to offer proof through direct observation. . . . I consider it my right and in a sense my duty to continue the cultivation of feminine feelings which are based on the presence of the nerves of voluptuousness. It is not base sensuousness which is at work in my case . . . but as soon as I am alone with God—if I may say so—it is a must for me to strive with all possible effort and to the full measure of my intellectual and imaginative capacities to convey to the divine rays the impression of a woman at the height of sexual voluptuousness.

The themes of sensuousness, nerves of voluptuousness, soul voluptuousness, voluptuous enjoyment, and their "close relationship to an everlasting state of bliss" fill many pages of the *Memoirs.*

The last chapter, XXII, contains a reaffirmation of Schreber's uniqueness and grandeur. He puts it thus:

The question may be raised whether I am at all mortal and what could possibly cause my death. From what I know about the restitutive power of the divine rays in my body, it is likely that ordinary illness and even violent external influences can be ruled out as possible causes of death in my case.

He repeats that his transformation into a woman is essential for the regeneration of mankind, and predicts the possibility that this regeneration will come about through divine fertilization with offspring issuing from his body. If, contrary to expectation, he should die, what then will become of God and mankind? In Schreber's opinion, God's attitude toward this Earth and to all human beings is derived essentially from His relationship with Schreber. In the improbable event of Schreber's death, overwhelming changes would of necessity follow.

On this note of megalomanic grandiosity, Schreber ends his autobiographical account. The remainder of the book contains various postscripts and appendices, legal documents concerning his release from confinement, and the forensic-psychiatric opinions of the hospital doctors pertaining to the case.

The foregoing excerpts from Schreber's book—incomplete as they are—provide a glimpse into the profound mental disorder from which the patient suffered. It is my opinion that the *Memoirs* offer the best account yet written of a psychotic illness as experienced by a person thus afflicted. For this reason, I have quoted many of the patient's self-revelations directly from his narrative.

As Freud had suggested, it would be useful for the scientific researcher to acquaint himself with the entire text of the *Memoirs*. The salient features of Schreber's psychosis are discussed and interpreted in the chapters that follow.

3 / Freud's Analysis

A Summary

Freud's Schreber analysis,[1] a work of great interest and lasting value, is composed of five parts: Introduction, Case History, Interpretations, On the Mechanisms of Paranoia, and Postscript.

After describing the essential elements of the case history and the course of Schreber's two illnesses, Freud delves directly into the substance of the *Memoirs*. He points to the high level of intelligence that distinguishes its author and then interprets the nature of Schreber's fantasies.

A study of these fantasies reveals that the idea of being transformed into a woman (that is, of being emasculated) was the primary delusion. Initially, Schreber regarded the act of emasculation as persecution and a serious injury, and only secondarily did it become related to his assumption of the role of the Redeemer. Freud explained that there could be little doubt that Schreber originally believed the emasculation was for the purpose of sexual abuse, and not in the service of some higher design.

The part of persecutor at first assigned to Dr. Flechsig (Schreber's first psychiatrist) was subsequently bestowed on God. In Schreber's words:

It was very natural . . . that I should view Professor Flechsig or his soul as my only true enemy . . . and that I should see in God my personal ally. . . . It was not until very much later that the idea entered my mind that God himself has been an accomplice, if not the instigator of the plot by which my soul was to be murdered and my body used like that of a whore. . . .

According to Freud, the emasculation fantasy was of a primary nature, originally unconnected with the Redeemer motif. The idea of being transformed into a woman was the salient feature and the earliest germ of Schreber's delusional system. This fantasy emerged prior to his second illness, before he had begun to feel the effects of heavy overwork after his promotion to *Senatspräsident* in Dresden.

It was only much later, in November, 1895, that the two originally separate fantasies coalesced in Schreber's thinking, as he himself reports: "Now, how-

[1] This is a condensation of Freud's "Psycho-Analytic Notes upon an Autobiographical Account of a Case of Paranoia (Dementia Paranoides)," which should be read in its entirety.

ever, I became clearly aware that the order of the universe demanded my emasculation . . . and that no rational course was available but to accept the thought of being transformed into a woman . . . ." Thus, Schreber became reconciled to this idea and his delusional system can be formulated as follows: I, Daniel Paul Schreber, am appointed to redeem the world and to restore it to its lost state of bliss. This, however, can be brought about only if I am first transformed from a man into a woman. After a long period of suffering which must precede the anticipated change, the glorious destiny of being impregnated by God will be attained. A better race of men will result, with a new and healthier generation issuing from my [Schreber's] womb.

In discussing Schreber's attitude toward God, Freud notes that throughout the *Memoirs* one finds the nagging complaint that God does not in fact comprehend living persons. Schreber thought God had become the instigator of the conspiracy against him, considered him demented, and submitted him to many torments. Of importance to the understanding of the case is Schreber's peculiar combination of worship and admiration toward God on the one hand, and opposition to and disrespect for Him on the other. In assuming a feminine attitude toward God, he believed he was God's wife.

Schreber was convinced that anyone who saw him standing before the mirror with the top part of his body naked, could not escape the impression of a female bosom, especially if he adorned himself with frills and other feminine accessories. He suggests that a medical examination will prove that his entire body is pervaded by nerves of voluptuousness which he believes to be characteristic of the female sex, since in the case of the male sex the location of these nerves is known to be only in or near the sexual organs as such. These nerves have created in his body a voluptuousness so intense that he can by the slightest use of his imagination produce in himself a feeling of sensual delight such as to provide a definite savoring of the enjoyment experienced by a woman in sexual intercourse.

The findings at which Freud arrived through his analysis of the *Memoirs* corroborated those of his previous studies. With specific reference to Schreber, Freud explains the mechanism of paranoia thus:

The exciting cause of the illness was the appearance of a feminine (that is, a passive homosexual) wishful fantasy, which took as its object the figure of his doctor. An intense resistance to this fantasy arose on the part of Schreber's personality, and the ensuing defensive struggle, took on that of a delusion of persecution. The person he longed for now became his persecutor, and the content of his wishful fantasy became the content of his persecution. The patient's struggle with Flechsig became revealed to him as a conflict with God. This is construed as an infantile conflict with the father whom he loved; the details of that conflict were what determined the content of his delusions. In the final stage of Schreber's delusion a magnificent victory was scored by the infantile sexual urge; for voluptuousness became God-fearing, and God

Himself (his father) never tired of demanding it of him. His father's most dreaded threat, castration, actually provided the material for his wishful fantasy of being transformed into a woman.

At the height of his illness, Schreber became convinced of the imminence of a great catastrophe, the destruction of the world. He felt that the earth's allotted span was only about 200 years more. During part of his stay in the mental institution, Schreber believed that the allotted period had already ended or that it was about to elapse. He himself was "the only real man still surviving," and the few human shapes that he still saw—the physician, the attendants, the other patients—belonged to the class of "miracled-up, fleetingly made little men." He had various beliefs regarding the cause of the catastrophe. During one phase of the illness, he thought it was due to the conflict between him and Dr. Flechsig; at a later stage, he believed it was brought about by the indissoluble bond which existed between him and God.

According to Freud, Schreber's idea of the end of the world was a projection of the patient's sense of an inner catastrophic alteration. The destruction of the world is the projection of this uncanny feeling of a devastating and pathological change within, caused by detachment of the libido from the representation of the external world (decathexis). The libido thus liberated is withdrawn into the self and is used for its aggrandizement (megalomania). This development is made possible by the paranoid's early fixation at the stage of narcissism to which he tends to regress.

A homosexual wishful fantasy of loving a man lies at the core of the conflict in cases of paranoia among males. The familiar principal forms of paranoia can all be represented as contradictions of the single proposition: "I (a man) *love* him (a man)." This is changed to "I do not love him—I *hate* him." Still unacceptable in this form, the feeling expressed in the second statement is projected onto the one originally loved. Consequently the proposition "I hate *him*" is transformed via projection into the idea "he hates *me*, and is persecuting *me*," such change providing the inner justification for "*hating him*."

The most important characteristic of symptom formation in paranoia is the process which deserves the name of projection. By dint of this mechanism, recognized by Freud long before the Schreber analysis, internal feelings, impulses, or ideas unacceptable to the ego are attributed to the environment; that is, something taking place within the patient enters consciousness as a disguised perception of the external world.

Repression is also connected with paranoia in the following three phases: fixation, repression proper, and return of the repressed. Freud explained that during the first stage of psychotic illness, the process of repression decathects the repressed mental representations of objects which, as a result, cease to exist. Hence, the psychotic patient's break with reality. The delusions and hallucinations which, in Freud's view, characterize the second or restitutive phase of the illness are attempts to recathect object representations, albeit in a distorted form. They are restitutional symptoms. Such restitutive attempts can be more or less, though never entirely, successful.

Freud's discovery of the role of unconscious homosexuality and the defense mechanisms in Schreber's pathology can be viewed as a breakthrough in the psychogenetic understanding of paranoid conditions. In analyzing Schreber's autobiographical account and elucidating the psychogenesis of his illness, Freud's work on Schreber's book represents a classic analytic study of the first order.

4 / General Comments on Freud's Schreber Analysis, the Memoirs, and Paranoid Personalities

Freud rested his interpretation of the *Memoirs* on his discovery of Schreber's homosexuality and its role in paranoid illness; the mixture of reverence and rebelliousness in Schreber's relation to God (father); the unconscious conflict and persistent love-hate duel that resulted, and the defensive and restitutive features typical of this type of psychosis.

He focused on that area of psychoanalytic research which has remained at the center of clinical analytic work: the investigation of libidinal and psychosexual development. He interpreted Schreber's illness and pathological productions within the confines of the analytic knowledge as of 1911. Since then psychoanalysis has, of course, progressed and undergone further development, much of which was initiated by Freud himself in his subsequent writings. After his analysis of the Schreber case, he extended his inquiries along metapsychological lines and began his studies of the ego, its structure, functions, and alterations. The formation and vicissitudes of the superego likewise came within the orbit of his investigations.

This advance, pursued and expanded by analytic researchers after Freud's death, has led us to the exploration of the dynamics of aggression, pathogenic object relations, pregenital and narcissistic character formation, early traumatic influences, and other aspects of ego psychology. The role of sibling rivalry in and superego reactions against homosexual and aggressive strivings in the etiology of paranoid conditions has also been investigated, especially with regard to narcissism and passivity. If in 1911 the emphasis was on the elucidation of libidinal drives in the structure and emergence of paranoid states, further methodical inquiry into the nature of Schreber's delusional and hallucinatory experiences has brought to light events that may be viewed as concrete building stones in the matrix of these pathological formations. It has thus become possible to reconstruct the infantile genesis of those bizarre productions which Schreber described—often in minute detail—as *divine miracles*. It will be shown in "Schreber: Father and Son" and "The Miracled-Up World of Schreber's Childhood" that these fantasies turned out to be *distorted memories of realistic experiences in his early life*.

Before presenting these newer findings, it seems appropriate to mention some of the frequent attempts made from various quarters to disprove or minimize the validity of Freud's work on Schreber. The ill-founded, usually abrasive remarks ("outdated" and the like) of such criticism frequently accompany the truism that the Schreber analysis was based on a printed autobiography and not on the spoken words of a living patient.[1] The authors of two recently published books (92, 110) assert that Freud wrote only "one case history about a psychotic . . . but never saw the man" and that Freud had only "limited or even indirect contact with paranoid patients." Such statements reveal a remarkable degree of ignorance not merely of Freud's publications on paranoia both before and after the Schreber analysis (30, 36, 39, 40), but also of the Schreber analysis itself in whose opening paragraph Freud reports that he sees "plenty of cases of paranoia and dementia praecox" in his own practice. Nor do these critics ever mention that the Schreber analysis, by virtue of its pioneering use of a printed text for analytic interpretation, became the precursor of many such subsequent efforts—not always successful—to penetrate the deeper meaning of biographical and non-biographical writings.

Freud had attacked the problem of paranoia at an early stage of his research in psychopathology and in his clinical work had come to see an unconscious link between latent homosexuality and overt persecutory delusions. He found in paranoia a mental disorder in which the underlying homosexual wish-fantasy—that of loving a man—is not at all obvious to the observer or conscious in the patient; the latter, on the contrary, strongly resists and defends against it, just as the great majority of members of the profession resisted Freud's theories at the time he published them. Thus, the study of the *Memoirs* offered Freud a welcome opportunity to apply his clinical-analytic insights to a document totally uninfluenced by his own observations, that is, to the self-revelations of a distinguished jurist who had been as unaware of Freud's work as Freud had been of Schreber's existence before his study of the *Memoirs*.

At one point in his research Freud was somewhat puzzled: in speaking of the soul murder committed on him, Schreber referred to Goethe's *Faust*, Byron's *Manfred*, and Weber's *Freischütz* by way of illustration. Freud could not find the expression "soul murder" in any of these works. Since "soul murder" is indeed not mentioned in any of the sources cited by Schreber, we shall have to rely, I believe, on Schreber's own text: in a passage at the end of Chapter V of the *Memoirs*, he equates soul murder with castration and, as a result of the emasculation, with the destruction of his reason.[2]

---

[1] It is of interest that other critics reproach Freud for *not* having investigated the printed works of Schreber's father.

[2] I am indebted to Dr. Donald L. Burnham for the information that the expression "soul murder" is used by Strindberg, whose essay "Själamord" (Soul Murder), originally published in France in 1887, also appeared later in the Swedish and German literature.

Schreber and Strindberg were contemporaries, and the latter's reputation in Germany was well established before Schreber's second hospitalization in 1893. In view of Schreber's avid reading and his wide knowledge of literature and languages, it cannot be

In some areas the Schreber analysis appears too "restrained," as Freud himself remarked. For example, the psychotic type of transference that led to Dr. Flechsig's deification, soon to be followed by his reduction to "little Flechsig," could have benefited from further elaboration. The same holds true of Schreber's dictum that God, by his very nature, is foremost "nerve." In my opinion, this statement, which appears in the first paragraphs of the *Memoirs*, likewise belongs to the psychotic transference phenomena in the complex Schreber-God-Flechsig relation. A glance at the photograph (see p. 112) of Dr. Flechsig, majestically enthroned in his office (in which he must have interviewed the patient Schreber) with a huge chart of the brain behind him and pictures and containers of nerve tissues at his side, can leave little doubt as to the meaning of these frank transference manifestations.

It was Freud's assumption that psychotic patients fail to establish transference. We know today that schizophrenics may develop unusual transference reactions to the point of transference psychosis—with disavowal of reality and greatly intensified dependence on the therapist. Such a development seems to have occurred in the situation between Schreber and Dr. Flechsig.

Paranoia and paranoid conditions are characterized by hostility, suspiciousness, persecutory ideas, perceptual distortions, regressive tendencies, expansive grandiosity, delusional thinking, excessive righteousness, and, in severe cases, a break with reality. The paranoid individual is easily slighted ("people are against me"). He sees himself persecuted by malevolent figures ("enemies"). He may become moody and depressed because he feels menaced by conspiratorial opponents, by "overheard" accusatory remarks, by "observed" inimical actions, and/or by hostile "plots" against him. He may counter the actual or inferred malevolence of the environment by resorting to such aggressive actions of his own as querulous and litigious modes of behavior, ill-advised legal (or illegal) procedures, secretive "counterplots" (to forestall a suspected conspiracy), or the like. When overwhelmed by paranoid fears, he may become either suicidal or homicidal, or both.

Speaking of paranoid thinking in metaphor, it may be of help to the nonprofessional to view the *modus operandi* in this way: every incident, every personal encounter passes through a filter of distrust and suspicion. The filter, of whose existence the paranoid individual is not aware, makes him see enemies who surround him, secret machinations directed against him, dangerous people who are out to "get him." The world thus becomes a perilous, hostile place, with him as the chosen victim.

Of paramount importance is the phenomenon of the paranoid personality's ascent to political leadership. Its impact on national and international affairs

---

ruled out that he might have found the term in Strindberg's writings. I am now in the process of searching for further material on this point. At present no certainty exists that Strindberg was a possible source of Schreber's use of "soul murder."

can be disastrous. It seems that under certain conditions the combination of power, grandiosity, isolation, secrecy, guardedness, inner insecurity, and relentless tension can set into motion paranoid tendencies long dormant in vulnerable individuals. It is this combination that is at the heart of what is known as the *nemesis of power*. When persecutory trends develop insidiously —that is, hidden from the environment and the person's own awareness— the paranoid leader may attribute sinister ("ulterior") motives to other people or agencies. He may become increasingly suspicious, secretive, un- compromising, resentful, irascible, moody, and seclusive. Preoccupied with inner conflicts and oversensitive to dreaded influences from without, his over- concern with maintaining or losing "control" (power) may expand into a rigidly fixed, paranoidally tinged "system" or crystallize in hatred against *one* person, a *group of persons*, a *people*, or a *country*. Recorded history offers countless examples of this kind. The realities of the political arena, which frequently involve a variety of behind-the-scenes maneuvers and activities, tend to add to the ever-present psychic tensions of the paranoid person in authority, thus reinforcing latent paranoid attitudes and persecutory ideas.

It should be kept in mind that a sensitive person whose presence and actions are constantly under public scrutiny is more apt to succumb to under- lying paranoid trends when exposed to relentless attack and implacable ten- sion.

Many such reactions are, of course, observable in perfectly sane people too, especially under conditions of stress and strain. In the paranoid indi- vidual, however, a marked increase in the frequency and intensity of these reactions occurs. Since the individual thus afflicted has previously demon- strated his efficiency and/or superiority, the gradual deterioration of his state of mind is likely to remain undetected over a period of time. Or, if recog- nized, the very position held by the paranoid ruler may make timely inter- vention impossible, particularly in a totalitarian setting. Again, history teaches that a paranoid leader in full political and military control, can rarely be unseated despite the environment's recognition of his mental con- dition.

Furthermore, the actions and pronouncements of a gifted paranoid leader lend themselves to evoking in his followers conscious and unconscious feel- ings of the same nature (hostility, hatred, distrust, scapegoating, jealousy). In this way he creates a strong common bond between him and the group under his control, with the result that national or even international disaster may become inevitable. The existence of large population groups that have incorporated the delusional convictions of paranoid leaders is a political- social phenomenon of the greatest import. Far from being completely under- stood, it requires the full attention of social scientists, historians, ethnologists, and psychologists—especially in our time. To attribute its frequent occurrence to socioeconomic stress alone, as popular explanations have it, over-looks the influence of less manifest, yet equally significant, factors.

In the exalted type of paranoia, ideas of grandeur may assume the form of missionary megalomania, religious or mystical beliefs of an overexpansive and overzealous character, feelings of being imbued or communicating with supernatural powers. The evolution of these fantasies into a fully developed paranoid system encompassing the individual, his milieu, and ultimately the universe—as in Schreber's delusional cosmology—requires superior intel-ligence. However irrational and repulsive the system may appear to the outsider, a sense of complete justification pervades the thinking of both the leader and his followers.

Convinced of the accuracy and righteousness of his beliefs the paranoid clings to them obstinately, fitting old themes of mistrust into the present framework of persecutory ideas and extending them constantly so that ulti-mately they dominate his entire mental life. Facts running counter to his convictions are dismissed with scornful disdain, often by adducing as "proof" those daily life situations which can be exaggerated or elaborated in such a way as to assign to them a persecutory meaning (personal slights, inadvertent omissions, irritating incidents). They provide the rationalization for the underlying hostility and allow the paranoid individual to "explain" his suspiciousness and anger in an apparently reasonable way.

As we have seen, many of these thought processes fill the pages of the *Memoirs*, which in a sense is a textbook of such symptomatology. This treasure chest of paranoid thinking also includes what in today's terminology is known as transsexualism. Doubt as to the sexual role is a common phenomenon in many psychiatric disorders. Schreber's thoughts circled again and again around the theme of his gender identity. He was a man who wanted to become a woman. Only toward the final stages of his illness did he reach this goal, partially solving his profound conflict. He reports proudly that he is in the possession of female sex characteristics and has "inscribed the cultiva-tion of femininity" on his banner. After arriving at this solution he was for a time generally content with his fate and at ease with himself and the en-vironment.

Consistent with this development are certain supplemental findings as-sembled in recent years. In 1972 I located and interviewed Schreber's adopted daughter in West Germany. The intelligent 79-year-old lady, in excellent physical and mental condition, supplied me with valuable information on Schreber's personality and behavior after his release from confinement. She was then a young girl, half-orphaned, and was adopted by the childless Schreber couple in 1903. She lived with them in their newly built home in Dresden until 1907 and vividly recalled her years there. Her adoption came about on the patient's initiative and, according to her description, Schreber was "more of a mother to me than my mother." She also gave me letters and poems written by Schreber, details on his personal warmth and kindness, told me how he helped her with her school work, took her on hikes through the forests and mountains surrounding Dresden, and so on. These additional data coincide with information from other sources.[3] Schreber's letters and poetry disclose his personal sensitivity and a quality of genuine tenderness, over and above that creative ability which found expression also in the writing of the *Memoirs*.

That Schreber as a father displayed more maternal feeling and behavior than the mother rounds out our picture of the subjectively desired self-transformation into a woman. In regard to the childlessness of the Schreber couple about which the patient complained in the *Memoirs*, I believe we are justified in concluding that childlessness played a significant role among the factors that culminated in the wish to become a woman. In his delusional thinking, the patient may well have felt that as a woman he might be able to do considerably better than his wife, that is, to produce healthy and living children, an achievement of which she had been incapable.

[3] I am especially indebted to Frau Prof. H. K., a direct descendant of the Wenck family (see Schreber genealogy, p. 4), who during my interviews with her in Freiburg, Germany, in 1969, 1971, and 1972 provided me with much valuable information.

5 / Paranoia and Its History

The history of paranoia and paranoid states is probably as old as mankind. The historical background cannot be understood without the insights of psychology and psychoanalysis.

What has been called the paranoid response appears to be linked to at least three basic elements in the human psyche: sexual conflict, fear, and the need for causality. We have already dealt briefly with the first two aspects. The factor of causality requires clarification.

The need for causality, an important function of the ego related to its synthetic function, has the compelling force of an instinct (86). When a young child stumbles over a stone and falls, he feels hurt and offended. His ego, far from accepting its own weakness and lack of muscular coordination as the cause of the injury, perceives the stone as the "bad" object, the evil-doer. In anger and revenge, the child may even attack and kick the stone, the "enemy." Melanie Klein traced the paranoid response still further back, to early infancy, and postulated internalized "bad objects" that function as internal persecutors.

Another example will illustrate the force of the causality factor. A hypnotized individual is given a posthypnotic order to go to the door, pick up an umbrella, and open it—in perfectly good weather. After emerging from the hypnotic state, he carries out the order. If asked why he opened the umbrella, he usually replies: "Because it is raining." The need for causality is so strong and urgent that, though the cause is lacking, it must in any case be supplied. *It is invented.*

This process has been operative in a great variety of forms throughout human history. The search for a real or imagined cause has led man to attribute disease, misfortune, failure, defeat, and death to such external agencies as moon, sun, devil, evil spirits, animals, and—other human beings. Through hundreds of millennia the attitude toward disease was based not on intellectual understanding; rather, it was a spontaneous emotional response to disability and pain. Physically, and above all, mentally ill people were far from being recognized as suffering from a sickness of the body or mind. Though we know little about the first stirrings of knowledge regarding these connections, the history of paranoia as a clinical entity can be traced to the

Hippocratic school, which flourished in ancient Greece in the fifth and fourth centuries B.C. Hippocrates distinguished several types of mental disorder, among them a form of psychic illness named paranoia, from the Greek *para* (beside, changed) and *nous* (reason, mind).

In its early application, the term meant disorganized thinking in its broad sense, that is, mental deterioration or aberration. Interestingly, though the literature on the subject is vast, the word or diagnosis *paranoia* was not used again for many centuries. There is little doubt, for instance, that the Roman emperor Tiberius exhibited symptoms that would be diagnosed as paranoid schizophrenia today. Because of his morbid delusion that danger threatened him on every side, he committed crime upon crime; yet his mental condition went unrecognized.[1] During the Middle Ages, religious and demonological explanations prevailed. With few exceptions, the medical vocabulary and symptomatology were expressed in religious terms. Although the Renaissance and post-Renaissance marked Western man's reorientation toward scientific observation and inquiry, it is important not to overlook the fact that the glory of the period was marred by the popularity of superstition and demonology. The blows of the *Malleus Maleficarum*, the "Witches' Hammer," the persecution and extermination of mentally ill people and other unfortunates *ad majorem gloriam Dei* fell into the same period of history that saw the splendors of Leonardo, Michelangelo, Titian, and Bellini. And it is worth noting that the highest authorities of the time (pope, emperor, universities) endorsed the burning horror expounded in the "Witches' Hammer."

Zilboorg views the persecution of witches as a mass paranoid psychosis that resulted from a severe conflict between the traditional authority of the medieval period and the awakening hedonism of the Renaissance. Sexual passions, theretofore consciously repudiated, were projected onto the external world and represented as attributes of the devil, an outside satanic force that collected all lustful "badness" imparted, via the return of the repressed, to human beings. The "Witches' Hammer" is replete with reports of *miracles* performed as *evil wonders* by people called witches. The licentiousness permeating present-day behavior and the frequency of political and racial persecution bring to mind the ominous psychology of those days.

A study of the history of paranoia demonstrates that it affects its victims regardless of their social status, religion, race, or country. Queen Juana *la Loca* (the mad one) of Spain, lived in seclusion, imagining herself and her environment to be possessed by evil spirits; often she would see a black cat tearing at her soul or that of her father. One of her successors, Charles II, was tormented by frequent visions of demons and other persecutors. Nor was the New World free of such beliefs. The burning of witches in Salem and the

---

[1] That timely detection could have helped is certainly doubtful. As mentioned earlier, history teaches that a paranoid ruler in military and political control can rarely be unseated.

lynchings of innocent people up to the present are too well known to require elaboration.

The famous M'Naghten Rule, of prime importance in the application of criminal law in both the United States and England for well over a century, goes back to the assassination in London in 1843 of Edward Drummond, private secretary to Prime Minister Robert Peel, by Daniel M'Naghten, a paranoiac. During the court sessions and through medical examinations it was established that M'Naghten imagined he was persecuted "by a system or crew that . . . followed him everywhere he went" and he was sure the crew was out "to kill him . . . as a part of the system that was destroying his health." In M'Naghten's disturbed mind, the person he shot was "one of the crew" that would kill him.

The mechanism of projection manifests itself with particular malignancy on the national and international levels where it usually takes this form: It is *they* who are greedy, untrustworthy, and rotten inside, not *we*. It is *they*, the "wops," "krauts," "gooks," "Japs," . . . *they* who kill, not *we*. A strong admixture of contempt—another form of aggression—almost regularly blends with such feelings.[2] The malignant aspect of all this lies in the strength and emotionalism of the conviction; its hold on the person's thinking is such that it is usually inaccessible to reason. No psychiatrist or psychologist, of course, claims that one can make definite inferences about the actions of groups or nations from the psychology of individuals. But the similarities are often striking and cannot be overlooked. Human nature, in particular that of decision-makers, is operative on all levels, including the national and inter-national.

As for spying activities or the belief of being spied upon—a regular ac-companiment of paranoid thinking and a grim reality in every totalitarian or quasi-totalitarian state—it is important to note that spying on parents and siblings is one of the most exciting pursuits in childhood. The witnessing of parental intercourse stimulates florid fantasy formation as well as extreme clandestine activities on the part of the child. With this background in mind, it becomes understandable that the pleasure of spying can pervade entire strata of a society, in particular a dictatorial form of government that, as a superego substitute, sanctions and rewards spying. The Hitler epoch in Ger-many (children secretly spying and reporting on their parents) and the Stalinist régime in Russia ("Doctors' plot") exemplify these massive contri-butions to the spread of paranoid attitudes in our time.

To return to the concept of paranoia, its use in the modern sense was reintroduced into the scientific literature by the German psychiatrist Karl Ludwig Kahlbaum, who, in 1863, thus designated the persecutory and

---

[2] As these examples indicate, the process of projection is not limited to paranoid states alone. It makes its appearance under a great variety of psychological conditions and generally influences our attitudes toward people and situations.

grandiose modes of ideation encountered in mental patients. Somewhat earlier, the French psychiatrists Esquirol and Lasègue had described paranoid thinking as *monomania* and *folie raisonante,* respectively. In Kahlbaum's classification, followed by that of Kraepelin, paranoia was listed as a separate clinical condition. Its existence as a separate disease has been questioned, and its occurrence thought infrequent. Most contemporary experts prefer to speak of paranoid schizophrenia or, in less severe disturbances, of paranoid reactions and states. The latter usually refer to a psychopathological disorder lying between paranoia and paranoid schizophrenia. There is no sharp borderline.

Since any rigid designation or classification of an illness tends to lead away from what matters most—that is, the human being as a suffering person—emphasis should be placed on the psychology of the individual thus afflicted: his personality, background, conflicts, relations, experiences, and motivations. To understand the delusional and hallucinatory phenomena experienced by such patients as Schreber, analytic investigation in depth is indispensable.

PART II

FURTHER RESEARCH ON SCHREBER

This part of the volume consists of a selection of my studies related to the Schreber case. All but one have appeared as contributions to various scientific journals. I have chosen to present these studies in the chronological order of their publication, since such an arrangement will indicate the gradual development of insight into the many complexities of the case.

In order to avoid inevitable redundancies, some articles have been amended, others abridged, and still others expanded as to content and clarification. Nonetheless, the substance of the articles as they appeared originally remains the same.

The important pictorial material is likewise reproduced here as in the original articles but has been supplemented by the addition of further illustrations.

6 / Three Notes on the Schreber Case[1]

Many years have elapsed since Freud's famous interpretation of the case (and close to half a century since the publication of the *Memoirs*). The subject has indeed become more familiar, and an attempt is made here to add some pertinent observations to the classic text.

1. THE ONSET OF SCHREBER'S TWO ILLNESSES

Schreber attributes the onset of his first two nervous disorders to "mental overstrain." I believe it important to investigate the circumstances under which these occurrences of "mental overstrain" developed. Although comparatively little is known about Schreber's first sickness—except that it is described as a condition of "severe hypochondriasis" and that it lasted several months, which the patient spent in a mental hospital—the time of its outbreak is well established. It began in 1884, when Schreber was a candidate for election to a post in the *Reichstag*, comparable to that of member of Congress in the United States or member of Parliament in England.

Since Schreber, at the onset of his first illness, was a candidate for an important political office, it is worthwhile to consider the political conditions then prevailing in Germany. Bismarck, the "Iron Chancellor," was then not only at the height of his power in the *Vaterland* but, as the highest official and chancellor of the Reich, was able to summon the *Reichstag* or dissolve it arbitrarily, as he had done repeatedly before 1884. It is important to note, for the understanding of Schreber's situation, that the dissolution of the *Reichstag* was generally recognized as a punishment and that the mere running for the *Reichstag* signified opposition to Bismarck, the undisputed father figure, who all his life had been against parliamentary ("filial") intrusion. If the *Reichstag* misbehaved toward Bismarck by voting against his policy, it was either threatened with dismissal or dissolved by him in short order and its members were sent home, much in the way a disciplinarian or

[1] Reprinted from *The Psychoanalytic Quarterly*, Vol. 20, No. 4 (October, 1951).

authoritarian teacher dismisses a misbehaving class in anger and paternal wrath.

We do not know exactly how Schreber's candidacy for the *Reichstag* came about, nor what became of it.[2] We do know, however, that it coincided with the occasion of his first illness, and as nothing has ever been said or written about the *Reichstagabgeordneter* (member of Congress) Schreber nor about an election campaign conducted by him, it is probably safe to assume that his candidacy may have ended by his withdrawal or defeat. In any case, it was at this time that his first illness made its appearance.

The second illness, of course, is known to us in detail, since Schreber's *Memoirs* as well as Freud's interpretation of them are almost entirely devoted to it. About the onset of this recurrence, Schreber states that it began after he was promoted to the high office of *Senatspräsident* (presiding judge) of the Superior Court of Appeals in Dresden. He fell ill at precisely the time he embarked on this new career, while preparing himself for the manifold duties and responsibilities of the important juridical post.

In light of these specific conditions, it is difficult to avoid the assumption that the two illnesses, both appearing under similar intrinsic circumstances, have a common denominator insofar as their precipitating cause is concerned. Moreover, there seems initially to have been little clinical difference between the two: in both instances the onset was marked by severe hypochondriacal symptoms that led to hospitalization. Before the outbreak of the second illness, Schreber dreamed two or three times that his old nervous disorder had returned. We thus learn from the patient himself that the two diseases appeared to him closely related; furthermore, he tells us that on each occasion a similar condition prevailed in his life, which he calls "mental overstrain," emphasizing "a very heavy burden of work" in the second. No further parallel between the two episodes can be drawn from Schreber's *Memoirs* about his situation at that time. It should be noted that he made suicidal attempts at the onset of both breakdowns.

Our question as to the immediate cause of both illnesses, then, reduces itself to a search for potential, precipitating factors that may have activated well-known latent forces in a paranoid individual, of which the patient himself— as so often happens in these cases—was not entirely unaware. His cautious generalizations about "mental overstrain" or "a very heavy burden of work" would seem, judging by their consequences, to refer to something more specific. What does he mean by them?

Primarily interested in the protracted second psychosis, Freud makes no mention of the onset or the meaning of Schreber's first illness. About the outbreak of the former, Freud draws attention only to "a somatic factor which may very well have been relevant" in the case and notes that Schreber

---

[2] This point is fully clarified in Chapter 10, which indicates that Schreber was defeated.

then "had reached a time of life which is of critical importance in sexual development—the climacteric." Apart from Freud's own doubts about this explanation, which recur throughout his text, and without distracting from the importance of the somatic factor emphasized by him, it seems to me that the possible action of such a somatic factor would explain only the outbreak of the second illness when Schreber was 51. It could hardly be regarded as a sufficiently active element in precipitating the first episode, which occurred eight or nine years earlier. Consequently, in accepting the "male climacteric" as a factor in the development of the second illness, one cannot possibly attribute to it the same significance in the earlier outbreak; nor does the presumed existence of such somatic factors preclude the importance of external events in the patient's life each time he became sick. In fact, if my view of the close connection and identity of Schreber's two illnesses is correct, it is impossible to avoid the assumption of such psychologically precipitating factors, which must have been operative on both occasions, or shortly before the onset.

From the study of Schreber's *Memoirs,* Freud concluded that in this case "we find ourselves once again upon the familiar ground of the father complex," as evidenced by the clinical picture, the patient's fantasies and delusions, and their analytic interpretation. This being so, we cannot fail to see that Schreber in his social relations with Flechsig, as well as in his delusions (God-sun-father) during his illness, succumbed to passive feminine fantasies only after having been put in the unbearable situation, before each outbreak, of assuming an active masculine role in real life, either by facing the father as the rebellious son or by becoming a father figure himself.

We may assume that Schreber's greatest dread was taking the place of the father. For reasons unknown to us, his marriage was childless though he apparently desired to have children. Under circumstances better known to us, however, we see that Schreber could not accept an active masculine role, in a wider sense. When called upon to become a member of the *Reichstag,* that is, a rebellious son in opposition to the awe-inspiring Bismarck,[3] he fell ill the first time. When, nine years later, he was called upon to take a father's place by becoming the presiding judge of the superior court, he again fell ill, and this time for good. Not being able to face the powerful father in fighting competition as a member of the *Reichstag,* or to take the place of father as *Senatspräsident,* he became incapacitated whenever such a threat appeared. Instead of running *for* office or accepting an appointment to a high office, he had to run *from* it, driven by his castration fantasies, which were set in motion the very moment the dreaded masculine role threatened to become a reality.

[3] There is an oblique reference to Bismarck in Schreber's book that possibly points in this direction: Bismarck, Goethe, and other great men belong to the "important souls" that later become higher, godlike entities.

How unbearable his position seemed to Schreber is stated in his own words when he describes, almost with insight, the dilemma in which he found himself as a result of his promotion in 1893:

This burden was the heavier, and put the greater demands on tact in personal intercourse, as the members of the five-man court, of which I had to assume the presidency, were nearly all my seniors, far superior to me in age (up to twenty years) and, moreover, more familiar with the practice of the court to which I was a newcomer.

The patient, in other words, found himself surrounded by threatening father-figures in whose midst he saw himself as a filial intruder, helpless and in danger.

Schreber, therefore, is completely right when, in referring to this situation, he speaks of "mental overstrain" and "a very heavy burden of work" to which he succumbed. We have only to add that the strain was not from overwork in the usual sense, but from the unbearable and overpowering burden coming, in 1884, from the threatening election or, in 1893, from the appointment to political (juridical) "masculinity." How much even the thought of an active masculine role was dreaded by Schreber is indicated by the fact that shortly after having been notified "of his *prospective* appointment as *Senatspräsident*," and some time before assuming this office, he had the ominous fantasy that ". . . it really must be very nice to be a woman submitting to the act of copulation." Under the impact of a threatening reality which imperiously demanded of him an active masculine role (this being precisely the situation he feared most, and which was consciously perceived as "mental overstrain" and "a very heavy burden"), his latent passive feminine tendencies broke into consciousness and he fell ill.

That, indeed, the same precipitating mechanism must have been at work nine years earlier, at the outbreak of the first illness, may be surmised from his statement about his repeated dreams that the former disease had returned. In the patient's unconscious the determining mental forces as well as their clinical results were obviously closely related. In fact, they were quite likely based on the same mechanisms and escaped from repression under virtually the same circumstances regardless of the presence or absence of an additional somatic factor.

Viewing the onset and duration of the two diseases in this light, I would like to venture a hypothesis about the different courses of the two illnesses. If they are similar in structure and origin, why did they have such different clinical courses, the one ending in recovery after one year, the other developing over years into an apparently lifelong process? I believe that here, in the protracted course of the second illness, the somatic factor resulting from the patient's age may play a part. We cannot, however, overlook the fact that the first relatively mild and temporary illness occurred in 1884 in connection with a political candidacy that, even if successful, would at best have resulted in a comparatively short period in public office. The second and lasting illness followed a promotion that under normal circumstances would have meant a permanent and practically irreversible life status for him. In this instance, a refusal would have been something like a crime, a kind of *lèse majesté* or worse, since such promotions were made by the king of Saxony, or at least confirmed by royal decree, and could not be refused. Illness, then, was the only way out, and with a lifelong position of this kind as a permanent threat before the patient, it could not be of short duration.

2. OBSERVATIONS OF A LINGUISTIC AND EXPLANATORY NATURE

Various obscure passages in the *Memoirs* appear unchanged and unexplained in Freud's study and have remained so, perhaps because they have not been deemed important enough to require further elaboration. I have noticed, however, that some of these difficult passages appear in the English translations of Freud's text and Schreber's book in such a manner that not only is their meaning lost, but sometimes actually reversed.

One of these passages deals with God's language, which in the German original as well as in Freud's monograph is called *Grundsprache*. In the English translations different versions are used; for instance, "root language" in the translation of Freud's paper or "basic language" in Fenichel's excerpts from the Schreber case. These translations are not only inaccurate; they may also miss an important point. When Schreber speaks of God's language as *Grundsprache*, it is well to remember that he was a learned and scholarly man, trained in philosophy and abstract thinking. He was certainly informed about such philosophical concepts of God as *Prima Causatio* or, in German, *der Grund allen Seins* ('ground and cause of all being'), and so on, with God recognized as the *Grund*, it becomes understandable that the language he speaks is the *Grund*-language. In fact, it may be assumed that to Schreber's way of thinking it has to be that way; it may well be that the "order of things" so often mentioned by him demands it. At any rate, just as a German speaks German and an Englishman English, it is only natural that God, the "Ground," uses *His* language, the "Ground"-language. Using such terms as "root language" or "basic language" makes this connection completely unintelligible for the English-speaking reader. There is still another reason why the word "ground" is particularly appropriate here, since it points the direction of Schreber's thinking. He also speaks of *Grundteufel* ("ground" devil) and certain *Untergrund* (underground) phenomena that, together with *Grundsprache* and other anal word usages, are characteristic of Schreber's trend of anal thinking and writing.

According to Schreber, on the one occasion during his illness when he saw God and heard him speak, a word was uttered that was current and forcible in the *Grundsprache*. This word was *Luder*. Translation of this unmistakable

German insult into "scoundrel," as the English version has it, is even more misleading. *Luder* is related to *liederlich,* the English "lewd," and clearly refers to a female. "Scoundrel" in German is *Schuft* or *Schurke,* referring only to males. The expression *Luder,* however, is a strong, antiquated, but often used insult in southern Germany (fitting perfectly into the *Grundsprache* described by Schreber as "a vigorous, somewhat antiquated German"), and is applied to a lewd female, a hussy, or even a whore. It is frequently used in combination with some other insulting epithet explicitly addressed to a female, such as *Dreckluder* or *Sauluder.* In current American slang, *Luder* might best be translated as "bitch" or "slut." Schreber, then, is called "tart," "bitch," or "slut," which in the context of the patient's delusional system is perfectly understandable.

Schreber states, in allusion to his emasculation, that the "rays of God" thought themselves entitled to mock at him by calling him "Miss Schreber." The word "Miss" is one of the very few English words that occur in the *Memoirs.* The question arises why Schreber should have used an English expression here. In certain parts of Germany the English term "Miss" had (and possibly still has) a definitely derogatory connotation. It designated an unmarried woman of somewhat doubtful reputation and character, who displayed an arrogance and ostentatious superciliousness. The meaning of "Miss" in the Germany of those days may best be compared with the use of *Fräulein* by American occupation troops there following World War II. Schreber himself makes it clear that his being called "Miss" can be understood only in this way. In the context in which he reports that the "rays of God" called him "Miss Schreber," he states that the voices, which are identical with the "rays," derided him and jeered at him. How did they do that? By calling him "Miss."

Completely incomprehensible in the English version are those passages that are repeatedly translated as "cursory contraptions." It is true that the original, *flüchtig hingemachte Männer,* is difficult enough to translate. But it is also true that the *flüchtig hingemachte Männer* of the original and the "cursory contraptions" or "fleetingly improvised men" of the translation have hardly anything in common, either in their wording or the ideational content. Schreber writes of *"men* cursorily made, drawn, or delineated," and not of contraptions. The full sense of these words remains doubtful, since no detailed elaboration is given by Schreber, who describes himself as being extremely puzzled by these phenomena. Freud believes they may refer to children or spermatozoa or a combination of both, and Katan has recently made a special study of Schreber's "little men."

The "ground language," properly understood, may contain the key to the meaning of these obscure passages. According to Schreber's statement, the expressions *flüchtig hingemachte Männer, kleine Männer, Luder, Grundteufel, Untergrund,* and so on, belong in one way or other to the "ground language." We are told by Schreber that this language is "a vigorous, somewhat antiquated German," and we also know from certain words of this language, like *Grund* or *Luder*, that it seems to be especially rich in expressions deriving from or belonging to anal terminology. Viewing Schreber's *flüchtig hingemachte Männer* in this way, and with the additional knowledge that *hinmachen* means not only "make" but also "defecate," and that, moreover, it is often used in the sense of "kill" or "murder," especially in southern Germany, it becomes evident that these frequent passages, obscure as they are, have to do with anal-sadistic word usages—certainly not too strange a finding in Schreber, who devotes page after page to the description of God's processes of evacuation and other anal activities.

This view is supported by a closer study of those chapters in the *Memoirs* in which the puzzling *flüchtig hingemachte Männer* are mentioned. In the early part of the book they frequently appear in connection with other expressions denoting "dead," "dying," "dissolved," "disappeared," and so on— that is, destroyed. In other passages the specifically anal meaning emerges even more clearly, for instance, when Schreber writes: "The orderlies M. and Sch. loaded a part of their bodies as a foul mass into my body in order to sit away." Schreber describes the noises that he heard repeatedly during the "sitting of the cursorily made men" as *röcheln*, which literally means "rattle" or "death rattle." In other passages he speaks of these phenomena as "being really souls," and he equates "being among fleetingly made men" as being "amongst the fossils," again a clear allusion to dead, destroyed, and anal objects. The expression "amongst the fossils" is especially characteristic of the "ground language": even literally speaking, fossils are ground objects; but in a further sense "fossils" refers to persons who are dead or whom one wishes dead, and was often used in German university circles in this sense. Schreber also speaks of the "little men" as having a repulsive odor, and as being of a strange color, described as *möhrenrot* (carrot-red), a very unusual and, I believe, unique German word. This Schreberian neologism, then, is understandable only in terms of the fecal brownish yellow color of the carrot as well as its shape, while red probably has the sadistic meaning of blood and killing.

A similar meaning emerges from a closer study of those passages in which Schreber discusses the "little men" in direct connection with specific persons. He repeatedly mentions the "little men" in close association with "little Flechsig" and "little von W.",[4] his two main persecutors. From the associative context and the choice of words, it has clearly the same anal-sadistic, paranoiac meaning.

There remains still another connotation not yet fully considered. The German *hinmachen* means not only to make, to defecate, to kill, but also to draw or to sketch. In the last sense, it may refer to those numerous diagrams, pictures, and drawings of male figures that illustrate the book *Medical Indoor Gymnastics*, written by Schreber's father. Some detailed passages in the

[4] One of the attendants in the hospital.

Memoirs about the "fore courts" of God, His "posterior" courts, upper and lower parts, and so on, read like graphic though distorted descriptions of the anatomical illustrations included in the elder Schreber's book. In addition, several paragraphs of the *Memoirs* are devoted exclusively to a discussion of drawing and sketching.

3. THE ASCENT FROM FLECHSIG TO GOD IN SCHREBER'S DELUSIONAL SYSTEM

Freud was particularly interested in the psychopathological process that brought about "the ascent from Flechsig to God," a process in which the figure of the physician Flechsig was ultimately replaced by the superior figure of God.

Without at this point going into the clinical details of Schreber's delusional system, I wish to indicate that this ascent can be clearly followed in the *Memoirs*. The intermediate steps of this development are presented by Schreber's chronology of the various delusional names belonging to this part of his delusional system.

Of this chronology, the last four items were demonstrated by Freud. The first four items are taken from the *Memoirs* to show the various intermediate steps in the production of Schreber's delusional system, which culminates in his characteristic Flechsig-father-God delusion. These stages in his delusion can be found in those chapters which deal with his distortion of the intimate relations between the Schreber and Flechsig families.

The diagram on page 47 shows the patient's delusional use of the presence of *Gott* (God) in the father's and grandfather's names and *Theo* (God) in the physician's name, for the deification of the ancestors and, via the psychotic transference, of Flechsig. It also illustrates Schreber's statement "I have parts of their souls in my body."

The successive delusions may best be understood in terms of Freud's analysis of the patient's psychotic thought process as an "attempt at restitution." One of the characteristic manifestations of this attempt consists in an effort to regain the lost libidinal objects (from which the cathexis was withdrawn) by reinforcing the cathexis of the verbal representations standing for the lost objects. Hence the prominent role played by verbal production in schizophrenia such as neologisms, verbigeration, word salad, etc. The outstanding libidinal object from which the cathexis is withdrawn in Schreber's case is the father. The verbal representation of his father—his given name, Daniel Gottlieb—is recathected, and it will be noted that in all the variations of the delusional names the word "God" occurs in one combination or other. Among them, *Fürchtegott* (fear God) is of special interest, revealing the patient's ambivalence, his fear of God as well as the threat he addresses to God.

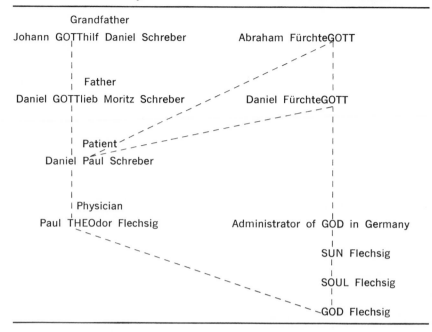

Ancestral Reality	Delusional Formations
Grandfather	
Johann GOTThilf Daniel Schreber	Abraham FürchteGOTT
Father	
Daniel GOTTlieb Moritz Schreber	Daniel FürchteGOTT
Patient	
Daniel Paul Schreber	
Physician	
Paul THEOdor Flechsig	Administrator of GOD in Germany
	SUN Flechsig
	SOUL Flechsig
	GOD Flechsig

It is noteworthy that the patient shared the name of Daniel with his father and the name of Paul with his physician. In the delusional system, the father's names, Daniel and Gottlieb, are bestowed on the physician with the various deifications, thus identifying him clearly as a representative of the father. Of the combinations Paul Theodor Flechsig, Daniel Fürchtegott, and Abraham Fürchtegott, Schreber states: "I have parts of their souls in my body." That from Theodor, literally "God's gift," Schreber draws on his knowledge of Greek is confirmed by him in several passages. The names Abraham and Daniel are of biblical origin, the former meaning "father of a multitude" and the latter, divine judge or judge appointed by God. It is a matter for speculation whether his use of the name Daniel, containing the Hebrew words *Dan* (judge) and *El* (God), is to be understood, as a double-edged threat, in the same double sense as *Fürchtegott*. At any rate, the deification of the father—a process for which the father's actual middle name, Gottlieb, offered a welcome opportunity—can be easily followed through its various, intermediate steps.

The father as such has vanished in consequence of the withdrawal of cathexis. His name, Daniel Gottlieb, however, has remained, and the cathexis it undergoes can in this system be identified point-blank, as it were, by following the various deifications. In this process the patient arrives step by step at the enthronement of Flechsig as God's administrator or proconsul in Germany, presumably a reference to Bismarck, and from there the cathexis of the word representations proceeds rapidly to culminate finally in "God." The process is now completed. First Flechsig, and then God, is reinstated in the place of father. With the new father, God, collecting the totality of cathexis, the schizophrenic thought process has gone as far as possible. It has run its full course in its attempt to restore, with the aid of verbal representations, those libidinal ties which had been abandoned.

7 / Schreber: Father and Son[1]

In studying the Schreber case I have previously limited myself to the *Memoirs*, Freud's famous monograph, and the subsequent contributions of other authors. I have since extended my investigations to include certain findings pertaining to the life and work of Schreber's father, the patient's ancestry, as well as the social milieu of his upbringing. Since, unfortunately, Chapter III of the *Memoirs*, which deals with Schreber's early family relationships, was deleted as "unfit for publication," and since very little else is said in the book about the author's childhood or adolescence, I pursued another route of investigation in an effort to learn the circumstances of Schreber's early life.

Having ascertained that Schreber's father had been a prolific writer, I reviewed as many of his printed works as I could find in the libraries and collections accessible to me, including several editions of the *Ärztliche Zimmergymnastik* (Medical Indoor Gymnastics). I also extracted data from published biographies of the father, as well as from unprinted biographical material gleaned from primary sources in Germany.

As almost fifty years have passed since the appearance of Freud's monograph and nearly a century since the elder Schreber's death, we are today in a position to deal more fully with the raw material provided by both father and son. Unhampered by Freud's need for restraint, we can endeavor to amplify certain of the analytic observations on the famous case by drawing directly from the father's publications. Some of these data enable us—as Freud had suggested—to trace numerous details of Schreber's delusions to their sources and to correlate a number of hitherto obscure passages in the description of his delusional system with particular ideas, principles, and the lifework cherished by the father. More specifically, I propose to focus attention on those correlations between paternal and filial mental productions that have not hitherto appeared in the psychoanalytic literature.

Daniel Paul Schreber was the second son of a social, medical, and educational reformer. The father, Dr. Daniel Gottlieb Moritz Schreber, was a physician, lecturer, writer, educator, and clinical instructor in the medical

[1] This is a slightly amended version of my original article, which appeared in *The Psychoanalytic Quarterly*, Vol. 28, No. 4 (Oct., 1959). The pictorial content is expanded.

school of the University of Leipzig. He specialized in orthopedics and later became the medical director of the orthopedic institute in that city. He wrote and had published close to twenty books on orthopedics and guidelines for rearing children. Reflected in these books was his especial interest in problems concerning the upbringing of children, physical culture, methodical body building through gymnastics, preventive medicine, school hygiene, and public health.

L. M. Politzer (89), who wrote a detailed, eulogistic obituary of Schreber, Sr., a few months after his death, called him "a physician, teacher, nutritionist, anthropologist, therapeutic gymnast and athlete, and above all, a man of action, of tremendous enthusiasm and endurance. . . ."

In describing the father's fame and work, Freud refrained from discussing the man's personality in detail. Nor did he mention his books, except for *Medical Indoor Gymnastics*. This was in conformity with Freud's "policy of restraint" explicitly stated in his monograph, a policy to which Freud both wisely and deliberately adhered while writing about the *Memoirs* of the younger Schreber. It is most likely due to this rule of restraint that Freud spoke of Schreber's father in the general terms that he did. Several of Dr. Schreber's children and members of his family, Professor Paul Flechsig, and others were still alive at the time of Freud's publication. It could hardly have escaped Freud's attention that there was more to this remarkable man, his character, influence, and work.

One of the popular books written by Dr. Schreber was published in Leipzig a hundred years ago. It is a guidebook for parents and educators. Its long-winded title reads: *Kallipaedie oder Erziehung zur Schönheit durch naturgetreue und gleichmässige Förderung normaler Körperbildung* (Kallipaedie or Education to Beauty Through Natural and Symmetrical Promotion of Normal Body Growth). Several equally verbose subtitles are added to the main title. After the author's death the book was reprinted; it was also called Dr. Schreber's *Erziehungslehre* (Educational Doctrination). I have chosen this volume for particular consideration because it deals almost exclusively with the upbringing of children from infancy to adolescence. Also, it contains passages that indicate that the methods and rules laid down by Dr. Schreber were not merely theoretical principles for the public, but were also regularly, actively, and personally applied by him in rearing his own children—with telling effect, as he reports with paternal pride. Indeed, he ascribes to his use of these methods a lifesaving influence on one of his offspring.

The main body of Dr. Schreber's educational system is condensed in his oft-repeated advice to parents and educators that they use a maximum of pressure and coercion during the earliest years of the child's life. He emphasizes that this will prevent much trouble in later years. At the same time, by subjecting the child to a rigid system of vigorous physical training and by combining methodical muscular exercises with measures aimed at physical and emotional restraint, both bodily and mental health will be promoted.

A detailed scrutiny of the book enables us to form some ideas about the early upbringing of young Daniel Paul and the general setting, emotional and otherwise, in which he grew up. Dr. Schreber seems to have been obsessively preoccupied with the posture[2] of young children, especially with active measures aimed at developing and maintaining the straightest possible posture at all times—whether standing, sitting, walking, or lying.

He constructed orthopedic apparatus to achieve these ends. In his instructions concerning the posture of children between two and eight years of age, he is very strict and demands that these children acquire and maintain a tensely erect posture. In another passage, referring to the same age group as well as to older children, the importance of an absolutely straight and supine posture during sleep is stressed. The reproduction of a few illustrations from the *Erziehungslehre* will serve better than words to indicate the nature of his educational methods and their forceful application by him.

Figures 1 and 2 show Dr. Schreber's apparatus for the enforcement of straight posture during sleep and its application *in situ*. Figures 3 and 4 illustrate the enforcement of straight posture in the sitting position by means of Dr. Schreber's *Geradehalter*. About the latter we are told by its inventor that "it is made of iron throughout . . . preventing any attempt at improper sitting. . . . It comes in two forms, one recommended for private use [in the home] and one, in more simplified form, for use in schools, particularly for the first two grades in elementary school." Later the *Schreber'sche Geradehalter* was modified by his friend and co-worker, Dr. Hennig, as shown in Figure 5.

Another of Dr. Schreber's body-building and muscle-strengthening inventions is the *Pangymnastikon*[3]—the whole gymnastic system condensed into one apparatus—the construction and application of which are described in his book of the same name. This device, ensuring that all gymnastic exercises are brought within the compass of a single piece of equipment, is viewed as the simplest means for achieving the fullest development of muscular strength and endurance.

A further important apparatus in Dr. Schreber's body-building system is the *Kopfhalter* (head holder) shown in Figure 6. Its purpose is to secure the symmetrical growth of the mandibular, maxillary, and related structures of the whole skull.

Many books by Dr. Schreber are filled with anatomical illustrations and numerous figure drawings showing the human body in a variety of positions, gymnastic exercises, and so on. In these drawings when the body is horizontal, the figure is usually shown to be rigid (Figure 7). The text likewise emphasizes both posture and endurance. Figures 8 and 9 show some of the anatomical illustrations contained in the books.

[2] It is likely that this preoccupation stems from the frail state of health that afflicted Dr. Schreber in his own youth. The biographical material contains a few oblique references to this as well as to his small stature. These circumstances may have contributed, I believe, to his great devotion to physical culture, calisthenics, fresh air, and so on.

[3] For further material on the Pangymnastikon, see p. 64.

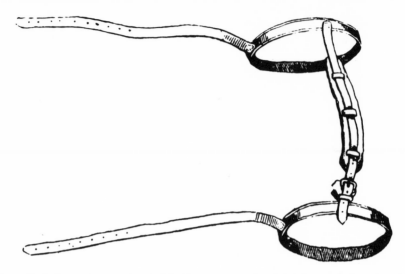

Figure 1 / Apparatus constructed for the purpose of maintaining perfect posture in the sleeping child.

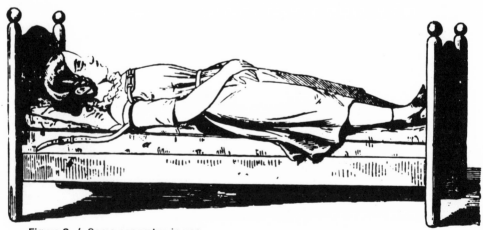

Figure 2 / Same apparatus in use.

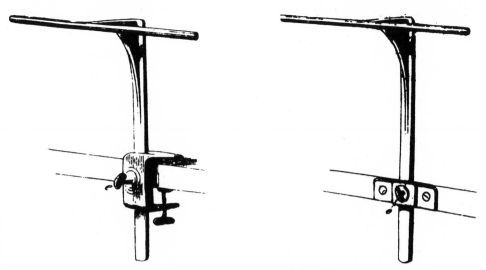

Figure 3 / *Geradehalter*, a device designed to ensure rigidly erect sitting posture.

Figure 4 / Practical application of the *Geradehalter*.

Figure 5 / *Geradehalter* with head belts.

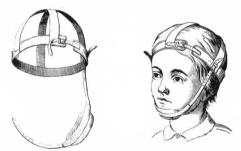

Figure 6 / *Kopfhalter* (head holder).

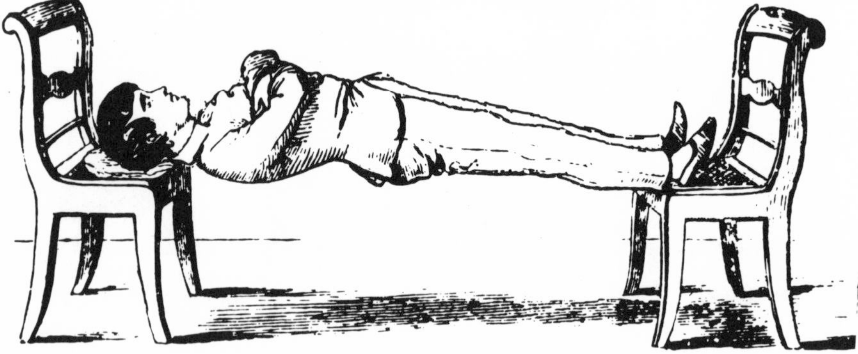

Figure 7 / Physical exercise, *Die Brücke* (the bridge).

54

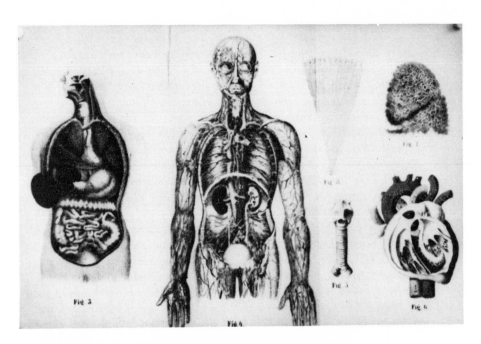

Figure 8 / Anatomical illustrations showing inner body organs.

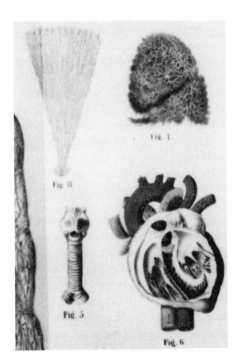

Figure 9 / Illustrations of individual organs: nerve fibers (upper left), pulmonary lobes (upper right), larynx and trachea (lower left), and heart (lower right).

Besides elaborate prescriptions for daily gymnastics and methodical calisthenics, in word and picture, we find in the *Erziehungslehre* detailed rules for every action during almost every hour in the regular routine of the child's life. There are minute, inflexible instructions for the child's total behavior, including its orderliness and cleanliness which "must be made the supreme law." Rules are specified for ritualistic, pre-breakfast or pre-lunch walking exercises with "no deviation allowed from the once established procedure," and with immediate punishment threatened if the child does not strictly conform. In such case "breakfast or lunch is to be withheld from it."

In a lengthy paragraph, "systematic and constant admonishments as well as exercises" are recommended for the proper pronunciation of words and syllables. Great care has to be taken that bad speaking habits, such as "smacking of tongue and lips, inhaling noisily through the nostrils, sniffing through the nose during the act of breathing are energetically put down." Equally to be combated are "the beginnings of passion," which from the very start require *direktes Niederkämpfen* (intense opposition or crushing). Disciplinary measures including corporal punishment are indicated at the slightest infringement and "at the earliest age . . . because the ignoble parts of the child's crude nature must be countered through great strictness."

Dr. Schreber then reminds his readers that they should never forget to compel the child, when it has been punished, "to stretch out its hand to the executor of the punishment"; this ensures "against the possibility of spite and bitterness." He recommends that a blackboard be hung in the children's room on which should be recorded each child's act of disobedience, forgetfulness, and so on, throughout the month. "At the end of the month, in the presence of all, a family session should be held" before the blackboard, and punishment or praise, as the case may be, should be given to each child on the basis of the marks and notes recorded. Finally, he assures parents and educators that the docility and submissiveness of children brought up in this fashion will be such that there will be no need for a continuation of this treatment after the fifth or sixth year of life; nor will parents have to worry, he adds in another chapter, about "dangerous, hidden aberrations," that is, that the child will masturbate later on.

To estimate the influence of such paternal precepts and disciplines on the son, it is well to bear in mind that a century or so ago similar notions were widely held, in medical and nonmedical circles, and we owe to Spitz's historical survey of masturbation a graphic description of such ideas. The very popularity of Dr. Schreber's books proves the point. Spitz points to the sadism "characteristic of the campaign against masturbation" during the second half of the nineteenth century and to the practices of mechanical restraint and corporal punishment that were given strong support by many authoritative physicians at that time. With due allowance to the *Zeitgeist*, it can nevertheless be assumed that the father's psychopathology as evidenced in his writings must have had a direct and massive impact not only on the public who held his writings in high esteem for several decades, but especially on his own family.

At least three biographical facts can be adduced to demonstrate the accuracy of this assumption. First, Dr. Schreber was a reformer who by his own admission drove some of his children, presumably his sons more than his daughters, into a state of complete submission and passive surrender. He made of them the earliest targets and examples of his aggressive efforts toward the development of a better and healthier race of men. Although the authoritarian regimentation of children with its emphasis on coercive disciplinary measures was probably typical of the country and the era in which Dr. Schreber lived, it is a matter of record that the straps, belts, and other forms of mechanical restraint were his personal inventions. They obviously sprang from his own pathology and were recommended and applied by him, though rationalized as educational reform. Certainly, some of his children were subjected to this "holy" purpose. In fact, the frequent exhortations in Dr. Schreber's books against the "softness" of life, the "decadence" of the world, and the threatening degeneracy of youth—his often repeated warnings and appeals to parents, educators, school and government authorities—in themselves indicate that such regimentation of children was even then becoming outmoded.

To the analytically trained observer, it is obvious that Dr. Schreber's energetic crusade was really directed against masturbation and other "dangerous, hidden aberrations," which in his thinking led to physical and mental "softness" in children. Indeed, at the time, this belief caused virtually all physicians and parents to dread masturbatory practices in their offspring. An arsenal of anti-masturbatory devices was therefore invented and applied not only by Dr. Schreber in Germany but also by others in various countries.[4] That Dr. Schreber's use of violent, sadistically tinged methods in this fight prevented at least one of his children from establishing an identity for himself, particularly a sexual identity, is recorded throughout the *Memoirs*.

The second assumption that there were strong sadistic components in Dr. Schreber's personality and behavior rests not alone on the material I extracted from his books. It receives direct support from an independent contemporary source. One of the medical reports on the patient, which Baumeyer recovered in Saxony some years ago, has an annotation that reads: *"Der*

---

[4] That masturbation in children had to be prevented at any cost was the accepted medical view during the Victorian era. Drs. William Acton (1813–1875) in England and Richard von Krafft-Ebing (1840–1902) in Germany, whose works were more popular than Dr. Schreber's, taught that virtually all perversions were the almost inevitable results of childhood masturbation. In T. S. Clousten's "Mental Diseases," a psychiatric textbook of wide circulation in the United States and England (in its fifth edition as late as 1898), the "habit of masturbation" is described as "very injurious to boys of neurotic temperament", and conducive to ". . . perverted emotionalism; depression; vacillation; cowardice; suicidal feelings; maniacal attacks; impulsive acts of violence, ending in Dementia in 26 per cent of the cases . . . ." Such thinking stimulated the invention of mechanical apparatus to protect the child against these otherwise "uncontrollable" consequences.

Vater (Schöpfer der Schrebergärten zu Leipzig) litt an Zwangsvorstellungen mit Mordtrieb" (The father, founder of the Schreber gardens in Leipzig, suffered from compulsive manifestations with murderous impulses). This illuminating statement contained in the medical report of the Sonnenstein Sanatorium, where the son was confined after his second breakdown, must have been based on information given to an attending psychiatrist in the sanatorium by some close member of the Schreber family, because the father had died more than thirty years before the entry was made.

The third biographical point refers to Dr. Schreber's death and what seems to have preceded it. According to his biographer, Ritter, Dr. Schreber suffered, probably in 1858 or 1859, a serious accident when a heavy iron ladder fell on his head in the gymnasium while he was performing his customary calisthenics. He seems never to have recovered fully from the sequelae of this injury described by Ritter as "a protracted, chronic head condition, the exact medical diagnosis of which is not known." The biographer then raises the question as to "whether actually this ladder accident or possibly a severe nervous breakdown" unconnected with the head injury may have been the basis of his illness. A letter written by one of Dr. Schreber's daughters to the Sonnenstein Sanatorium in 1900 also mentions "the fall of an iron ladder in the gymnasium on the head [of the father] some months before the onset of a strange disease of the head," and she hints that there were some marked changes in the father's character. At any rate, the cautious wording "strange disease of the head" and Ritter's outspoken allusion to a breakdown seem to indicate a mental illness, or at least an undiagnosed illness accompanied by prevalently mental symptoms, when the father was 50 or 51 years old. He died—and here we have the clinical diagnosis and the date—of intestinal ileus on November 10, 1861. A later autopsy revealed a perforation of the intestines in the area of the appendix.

In comparing the data about the illnesses that afflicted both father and son as each of them entered the sixth decade of life, and reviewing further the characteristics of certain mental productions of both men, it becomes difficult to avoid the recognition of some noteworthy similarities in the two. The father, following an injury to his head, falls ill in his fiftieth or fifty-first year with what his daughter and biographer alike call a strange disease of the head (*Kopfleiden*). He dies at the age of 53. The son, Daniel Paul, also becomes sick at the age of 51 and, initially, his chief symptoms are complaints about his head, softening of the brain, and fear of imminent death. In November, 1893, he is admitted, with his second and chronic disease, to the Leipzig University Psychiatric Clinic where, in that same month, he makes a suicide attempt. Two years later, when he has reached the age of 53, he records in his *Memoirs* a marked deterioration of his condition in these words: "The month of November, 1895, marks an important time in the history of my life. . . . During that time the signs of transformation into a woman became so marked on my body that I could no longer ignore the imminent goal at which the whole development was aiming. . . ."

Though the sick son does not explicitly say so in this passage, we know that the development of which he speaks was aiming at the union of himself, as a woman, with the deified father. At the age of 53, he connects this delusional goal chronologically with the month of November, the month his father died at 53. On further scrutinizing the medical reports, one notes that the three important hospitalizations in the younger Schreber's life occurred in or about the month of November, in different years of course, but all because of rather acutely developing mental symptoms necessitating his hospitalization just then. To be sure, coincidental factors cannot be ruled out; nor can it be ignored that the onset of the first two illnesses leading to hospitalization followed, on each occasion, those external life events which are discussed in some detail in the foregoing "Three Notes on the Schreber Case."

But had not the father's mental difficulties and overt nervous symptoms also followed an external event in *his* life, namely, the sudden head injury in the gymnasium? Could not then those external events in the son's life, especially his rather sudden and emotionally highly charged promotion at the age of 51, have been unconsciously equated by the patient to the very "blow on the head" that struck the father with such deleterious consequences at approximately the same age? In his *Memoirs,* the son time and again speaks of all sorts of blows directed at his head, often in connection with noise and spoken words.

Be that as it may, there are yet other factors to consider with respect to the introjected paternal image that remained enshrined in the son's ego and whose release can be traced in part through the chapters of his *Memoirs.* In one of the very few passages in which the son refers directly and in undistorted fashion to his father's work, he mentions the *twenty-third* edition of the paternal *Ärztliche Zimmergymnastik.* It is of significance that the *Memoirs* consist of precisely 23 chapters, including the introduction, and not counting the various postscripts and addenda. The finished manuscript of the *Memoirs* was handed to the Saxonian Court of Appeals (which had to decide on his release from the mental hospital) in precisely 23 copybooks written by the younger Schreber; he countered one of the main objections in court against their publication with the following pointed argument recorded in the legal proceedings: "The publication of the *Memoirs* is planned, according to preliminary agreement with the publisher Nauhardt in Leipzig, in the form of a contract on the basis of a commission, *the same form of publication in which the father's Medical Indoor Gymnastics appeared . . .*" (italics added).

The elder Schreber's *Erziehungslehre* was expressly dedicated to the welfare of future generations. Just as his writings were prompted by a missionary zeal to spread information on physical health and body building everywhere so that a stronger race of men would result, so the son, during his illness, appears to have been driven by the introjected paternal image in the direction of those same aspirations. In the introductory remarks to and in various chapters of the *Memoirs*, Schreber expresses his certainty that the publication of his experiences of miracles, God, rays, and so on, will be a blessing to humanity. His sole aim, he declares, is to spread truth and further knowledge for the good of mankind. The father, with no little apostolic grandeur, strives for the development of better health and hygiene in an earthbound way, as it were; the son in his delusional elaboration of these precepts does so in an archaic, magical way. The father's books are replete with anatomical illustrations and figure drawings. The sick son, during the years of hospitalization, often draws human figures on paper and fills pages of his own book with ruminations on drawing and sketching.

Throughout the *Memoirs* there are numerous references to God's "writing-down-system," which the patient himself finds "extraordinarily difficult to explain to other people . . . as it belongs even for me to the realm of the unfathomable." I am inclined to trace the origin of this divine "system" to the father's handwritten notes, manuscripts, books, and lectures. I also see in it the psychotic, regressively deified elaboration of the paternal blackboard, which, with its ominous marks and notes, probably played such a menacing role in the patient's childhood. It is to this "writing-down" method originally used by the father and later taken over by the son that we owe in some measure the appearance of the *Memoirs*. Long before Schreber began to write the full text, he kept notes in shorthand, jotted down his thoughts and experiences on scraps of paper, and later made annotations in copybooks. Had he not made ample use of "God's writing-down-system," the *Memoirs* might possibly never have been published, at least not in their present form.

It seems permissible, therefore, to think of the *Memoirs* as representing the younger Schreber's complex struggle for identification with his father as well as his battle against it, a struggle that accompanies and intensifies his homosexual conflict, so clearly elucidated by Freud. With this premise we can attempt to arrive at a fuller understanding of those bizarre ideas in the son's delusional system that, directly or indirectly, appear to be derived from the introjected paternal image, and that constitute archaic elaborations of certain paternal characteristics and procedures, as experiences introjected early in life and later "released" in the *Memoirs* by the son. The introjection of his autocratic father's methods re-emerge as delusional or hallucinatory entities in the son's archaic regression and he records them in a number of autobiographical, relevant, but otherwise obscure passages throughout the *Memoirs*. Many of the divine miracles of God affecting the patient's body become recognizable, shorn of their delusional distortions, as what they must originally have been modeled on: the infantile, regressively distorted image of the father's massive, coercive, as well as seductive manipulations performed on the child's body, as represented in Figures 1 through 7.

The father's apparatus of belts and body straps give new sense and meaning to such divine miracles as "being tied-to-earth," "being tied-to-celestial-bodies," or "fastened-to-rays." The "chest-compressing-miracle," described in the *Memoirs* as one of the most horrifying assaults against his body, also becomes clearer if viewed in its relation to the paternal apparatus shown in Figures 3 and 4.

The "coccyx miracle" repeatedly mentioned in the son's book refers, I believe, to the strict rules for sitting down enforced by the father. The seductive character of these paternal manipulations is clearly shown by the expression *"Menschenspielerei"* (play-with-human-beings) that Schreber connects, even in his preface, with the miracles and the stimulation caused by them.

Other miracles during the early years of hospitalization affected the son's "whole abdomen, the so-called *putrefaction of the abdomen*," caused the *"obstruction of my gut,"* and apparently gave him the feeling of "being dead and rotten" (italics in the original). These seem to refer to the shocking impact of the terminal ileus to which the father quite suddenly succumbed. The very night of his death the father had been scheduled to lecture before the Leipzig Pedagogical Society. The son was then 19 years of age.

As is well known in the case of other psychotic patients, Schreber was by no means without insight into some of these connections. About his identification with the father he states for example: "God is inseparably tied to my person through the power of attraction of my nerves. . . . There is no possibility of God freeing Himself from my nerves for the rest of my life." In another passage he writes: "I had the 'God' or 'Apostle' . . . in my body, more specifically in my belly." Note that the word "apostle" is used directly here by the son. In German idiom, the father was a *Gesundheitsapostel* (health apostle).

Of particular interest in the father's *Erziehungslehre* is the emphasis on early and massive bodily stimulation (through manipulations, exercises, appliances, and braces), which, at a somewhat later age, is combined with religious observations and practices. The child should be taught, Dr. Schreber explains, to turn "its mind to God at the end of every day, to review the feelings and actions of the day . . . in order to mirror its inner self in the pure rays of God, the loving and universal father. . . ." Dr. Schreber also recommends the mandatory teaching of human anatomy in direct conjunction with religious education in public schools. Several italicized pages in the concluding chapters of the *Erziehungslehre* deal in a rather obscure and mystical way with *dem rein Göttlichen* (the purely divine) and with the merging, in truly religious feeling, of two types of *Strahlen* (rays) to a point of complete union. Whether these notable passages in the father's work formed a sort of starting point for their later elaboration by the son into the equation *rays = father = God,* and also into the Schreberian divine hierarchy with its florid anatomical-religious peculiarities is difficult to decide, though I am inclined to see here too important interrelationships that invite further investigation.[5]

After having clarified the meaning of some of these obscurities in Schreber's *Memoirs*, we may come to understand more fully a few of his frequent complaints. When he protests, for instance, against "the enormous infringement of man's most primitive rights," or when he accuses Professor Flechsig ("you, like so many doctors [father], could not completely resist the temptation of using a patient as an object for experimentation"), we may legitimately connect the feelings here expressed with the massive coercive aspects of his early upbringing. By way of pointing more sharply to the patient's own wording, I am also inclined to see in these statements a confirmation of my earlier stated view that Dr. Schreber, the father, physician, educator, and reformer, quite likely chose his male children as objects for his reformatory "experimentation," as the son so aptly puts it. In fact, the first son, Gustav, committed suicide; the second son, Daniel Paul, became psychotic. The three daughters apparently remained well. This outcome, completely unknown to Freud, essentially corroborates his main thesis about the case.

Freud who presumably had no information about the patient's childhood nevertheless discovered from the *Memoirs* that their author must have found "his way back into the feminine attitude which he had exhibited toward his father in the earliest years" of his life. Freud also postulated on purely theoretical grounds that the brother might have been older than the patient. We now know that Freud was correct on both counts.

These data have thrown new light on certain peculiarities in Schreber's delusional system. In reconstructing and retracing the early elements of this case history, our next task will be to focus further attention on the early traumatic relationship with the father, on the nature and genesis of the divine miracles, and on the meaning of the cosmic myths common to both father and son.

[5] For a fuller discussion, see pp. 98ff.

8 / Schreber's Father[1]

Schreber's father, who as God became the central figure in the son's delusional system, was a person of unusual character and propensities. The official biographies, though hardly usable for analytic investigation because of their lack of childhood data and early family relationships, abound in laudatory descriptions of their subject and use language far transcending the customary hero worship of such chronicles. One of these biographers, A. Ritter, virtually deifies his subject, albeit in a nondelusional way. L. M. Politzer describes him as a great leader and pioneer, attributing to him the courage, strength, and enthusiasm of a religiously inspired fighter for all the "higher things" of life and arrives at this conclusion: if every century and every country were to produce such men as Schreber, mankind would not have to fear for its future.

Reducing these exuberant comments to somewhat more moderate proportions and summarizing the older biographical material on Dr. Schreber briefly, we can say that he, besides being a distinguished physician, was

1. A reformer thoroughly and apparently fanatically dedicated to his goals in the fields of physical culture and health.

2. A personality of great and lasting influence, as well as the founder of a cultist movement that survives to the present time.

On the basis of the recently discovered material discussed in the foregoing pages, we can add to this the further fact, not entirely unexpected by analysts, that

3. Dr. Schreber was a sick man.

About the father's childhood and adolescence we know very little. He was the second son of the Leipzig lawyer Daniel Gottfried Schreber and his wife Friederike, née Grosse. His elder brother Gustav had died at the age of 3. The only childhood experience reported by Ritter refers to a visit of the 5-year-old boy with his father to the battlefield near Leipzig where Napoleon,

---

[1] This is an abridged version of the original article, which appeared in the *Journal of the American Psychoanalytic Association*, Vol. 8, No. 3 (July, 1960).

after his flight from Russia, had suffered a crushing defeat. The young Schreber was searching for bullets and war trophies on the battlefield. This isolated memory may not be without some psychopathological significance. It is worth noting that after his graduation from medical school, at the age of 25, he became the personal physician of a Russian aristocrat and traveled with the latter extensively in Russia.

As an adolescent, it seems Schreber was a rather disturbed young man. One of his books contains a brief case history entitled *"Geständnis eines Wahnsinnig Gewesenen"* (Confessions of One Who Had Been Insane). This report, which Schreber attributes to a chance acquaintance he made during his early travels, is filled with vague allusions to attacks of melancholia, morbid brooding, and tormenting criminal impulses. In its veiled language the account reads like an autobiographical record the content of which corresponds essentially to the previously mentioned entry in the Sonnenstein report.

Dr. Schreber was a man of small stature, in his youth physically under-developed and of delicate health. Through persistent training, great personal effort, and methodical muscular exercises, he succeeded in becoming a robust man, "one of the best and most elegant athletes [of his time]. . . . This was the starting point for his writings and his endeavors for others in the field of physical culture." (91) The unconscious forces behind the man's relentless aspirations for the acquisition of better health through physical exercises and other body-building procedures are rather neatly, if tangentially, stated here. At the age of 50 or so, Dr. Schreber was the victor in an athletic contest in Karlsbad over much younger competition. Ritter tells us that Schreber him-self "was the model for the illustrations of his *Pangymnastikon,* since con-stant training had given his body perfect beauty."

Most of my information regarding the elder Schreber's personality, how-ever, comes from his own writings. He was the author of numerous books and booklets, many of them popular texts dealing with human anatomy and physiology, questions of hygiene, physical culture, and health education. For reasons of brevity, and also because it deals with Dr. Schreber's methods for the upbringing of young children, I refer once again to the *Kallipaedie,* or *Erziehungslehre.*

Expressly dedicated by the author to the "Blessing of Future Generations," the volume is replete with exhortations to parents and educators to apply Dr. Schreber's educational ideas and methods. Throughout this book and many of Dr. Schreber's other writings, great stress is laid on a proper postural system, strict obedience, prevention of "bad habits," and total and constant supervision of all aspects of the child's daily life. His upbringing must be regimented in rigid accordance with rules governing virtually every activity. Sleep is allowed only in a flat-on-the-back position, and Dr. Schreber invented a complex system of belts, straps, and body-straightening apparatus, the so-called *Geradehalter*, to ensure such a position in the sitting, walking, and sleeping child.

As an orthopedist, Dr. Schreber undoubtedly had frequent occasion to observe and treat physical deformities. In fact, some of his earlier books deal with diseases of the spinal column and their prevention. It should be recalled that orthopedic surgery as it exists today, was unknown during the period that Dr. Schreber practiced medicine. A good orthopedist had to rely on corrective devices and exercises.

In 1844 Dr. Schreber became the medical director of the Orthopedic Institute in Leipzig. He had originally intended to establish and manage a pediatric institution, but was prevented from doing so by the local health authorities, which were in opposition to his "highly independent and very strong-headed plans." Several passages in Dr. Schreber's texts lead me to conclude that he was in the habit of applying to, or at least testing on, his male offspring the orthopedic procedures that served him in his professional work with deformed children, thinking of these procedures as prophylactic measures against the development of possible deformities.

With the missionary zeal of the reformer, he seems to have expanded these originally limited orthopedic methods into a general system of physical culture as his means of promoting health through a nation-wide adoption of such practices. He kept adding further disciplinary, moral, and religious ideas to his hygienic-therapeutic principles, combining them into a regimented educational system for the use of parents and teachers everywhere so that they became virtually a way of life. It is perhaps not surprising that Schreber's biographer Ritter, expressing his admiration for both Schreber and Hitler, sees in the former a sort of spiritual precursor of Nazism.

To return to the *Erziehungslehre*, Dr. Schreber's educational principles directed toward radically crushing "the child's crude nature" from the earliest age, by means of verbal admonishments, mechanical restraint, and bodily punishment, can achieve, in his view, a state of complete submissiveness in all children before they reach their fifth or sixth year of life. Monthly family sessions for the purpose of sitting in judgment on the child's violations and misbehavior meticulously recorded on a blackboard, is another method strongly recommended. In his book, Dr. Schreber mentions the excellent results obtained in his own children through the use of this particular educational tool.

Turning to the influence of these paternal precepts on the son Daniel Paul, I am far from ascribing to the monthly court sessions before the paternal blackboard the fact that he later became a judge. Nor do I suggest that the son's pathology is rectilinearly derived from that of the father. I have already shown, however, that the massive impact of such paternal teaching, acting, and coercing can be traced in detail through the various chapters of the *Memoirs*. And I wish here to draw attention to the peculiar, sermonizing, and high-flung style of writing, to the exalted mode of addressing the readers with solemnity and aplomb, to the frequently stated goal of spreading information and knowledge in the interest of and as "a blessing" to mankind. These features are characteristics common to the writings of both father and son.

In addition, we find in the *Memoirs* a number of passages that read like distorted, archaically elaborated descriptions of the paternal ideas and procedures in the fields of education as well as orthopedics. Certain "divine miracles," for instance, which were performed on the author of the *Memoirs* during his illness and especially those in which his body was tied up, fastened, roped, and compressed as in a vise, seem to represent the son's delusional elaboration of the orthopedic straps, belts, holding apparatus, and other coercive devices used by the father. It also seems to me that God's "writing-down-system," which appears as a threatening and mysterious entity in various chapters of the *Memoirs,* has connections with the paternal blackboard and similar methods of control to which Schreber junior was subjected. Likewise the oft-mentioned "bellowing miracle" shows certain relations to the father's relentless exhortations as well as to the son's attempt at fighting back with equal if helpless vigor. The frequent occurrence of the expression *"geprüfte Seelen"* ("tested souls") in the *Memoirs* may ultimately refer to the father's habit of examining his children closely, testing their physical and mental endurance, checking on their posture and the effectiveness of the orthopedic appliances. The need for such "testing" on a regular basis is stressed in many of Dr. Schreber's texts.

Of great interest are the identification aspects of the Schreber case. The son shared his first name with his father and grandfather (Daniel), his middle name Paul with his mother whose first name was Pauline. Both father and mother were the descendants of distinguished professional families whose members on both sides alternated mainly between the legal and medical professions. Interspersed, were scientists and authors of scientific writings. All this crystallized in one way or another in Dr. Schreber's own writings, which, in turn, are delusionally reflected in the son's literary production.

Dr. Schreber died at the age of 53; the son fell ill with his second and protracted disease which made him feel "dead and rotten" at approximately the same age. He thought of himself as suffering from general paralysis and demanded "the cyanide destined for me." This frequent request for potassium cyanide or strychnine had long puzzled me until Baumeyer's supplementary data on the Schreber family came to my attention. As I have mentioned, the author of the *Memoirs* was Dr. Schreber's second son. The older son, Gustav, three years the patient's senior, committed suicide in 1877. Though we know even less about his development than we do of his father's, it would appear that this Schreber, too, was far from stable. At first, it seems, he became a chemist, only to change over to jurisprudence. It is certain that Gustav was a magistrate at the time he committed suicide. There was a question of whether he had been suffering from general paralysis before his death. Although the manner of his suicide has not been established,[2] the fact that this elder brother was a chemist may be significant.

Moreover, if we remember from the *Memoirs* the peculiar division of God into two distinct.persons, an upper and a lower God of different characteristics and appearance, it becomes likely that the figure of God in the second son's delusional system is a composite one: consisting of the superior person of the father as the upper God and of the inferior or successor figure of the brother as the lower God. Added to this composite figure of the deity are maternal attributes relating to the patient's mother.

[2] After I wrote this article, I ascertained that the suicide was committed by means of a self-inflicted gunshot. (See p. 97.)

9 / The "Miracled-Up" World of Schreber's Childhood[1]

In his study of the *Memoirs,* Freud formulated one of his main findings in these words: "Here we find ourselves . . . on the familiar ground of the father-complex."

Indeed, as it is the father who, transformed into the superior figure of God, stands in the center of the son's delusional system, and as it is also the father whose character and influence can now be more fully appraised on the basis of our additional background material, it may be expected that some heretofore inaccessible formations in Schreber's delusional system, especially those directly derived from the father-son situation, will now become analytically and genetically comprehensible.

This approach, with all its unfortunate lack of maternal data, appears even more promising in the light of Schreber's own statements that he is primarily concerned with "the relationship between God and myself" and with ideas formed by him as a result of his "impressions and experiences about . . . the essence and attributes of God. . . ." In the following pages, these paternal "essence and attributes" as well as "the *lasting* conditions" (italics in the original) caused by them in the son will be further investigated.

A RECONSTRUCTIVE SURVEY OF SCHREBER'S EARLY EXPERIENCES

If there existed a biographical outline of Schreber's life before he fell ill at the height of an impressive professional career, it would be relatively easy to give an anamnestic account of the events that ultimately led to his hospitalizations (and eventual death) in an insane asylum. As yet, no such account is possible. What is known adds up to few reliable, albeit relevant data on his childhood. From Baumeyer's report we learn that Schreber had been a brilliant student at school and that his memory always was and remained "excellent" through all the years of his illness. We learn further that the patient had shown "a hasty, restless, nervous nature . . . from childhood on," as reported in a letter by Schreber's youngest sister in 1900. This letter also

[1] This is a slightly amended version of the original article, which appeared in *The Psychoanalytic Study of the Child,* Vol. 14 (1959).

stresses her brother's rich intellectual gifts and his goodhearted, friendly personality. No further objective data about the patient's early life are available except that the Schreber family were devout Protestants and lived in comfortable economic circumstances.

In one of the few passages of the *Memoirs* in which the patient himself refers directly to his childhood, we are told:

Miracles of heat and cold were and still are directed against me . . . always with the purpose of preventing the natural feeling of bodily well-being. . . . During the *cold-miracle* the blood is forced out of the extremities, so causing a subjective feeling of cold . . . during the *heat-miracle* the blood is forced towards my face and head. . . . *From youth accustomed to enduring both heat and cold, these* miracles troubled me little. . . . (Italics added.)

These and other remarks induced me to inquire more closely into the nature and genesis of the "divine miracles" performed upon Schreber's body. Since one set of miracles is recorded here by Schreber in connection with a childhood reminiscence, I shall return to this point later. The quoted passage provided me with specific evidence concerning the reality of certain childhood events or experiences that may have played a role in the production of such fantasies. In recognition of the importance of the "historical truth" for the origin of many of these phenomena, I determined to submit the life and character of Schreber's father to further scrutiny in an effort to trace, if possible, the early history of the paternal contributions to the son's psychopathology. My investigations along these lines revealed relevant, scattered childhood material in the father's printed works. Several of his books offer lengthy descriptions of the particular methods and educational procedures used by him in the upbringing of his children. These have been described in part in preceding chapters.

Apart from a regimented, rigidly disciplined type of education, which seems to have been Schreber's lot from early infancy, he appears to have been forced into complete submission and passive surrender by a father whose sadism may have been but thinly disguised under a veneer of medical, reformatory, religious, and philanthropic ideas. Dr. Schreber invented unusual mechanical devices for coercing his children, presumably his sons more than his daughters, into submission. On the basis of ample evidence in Dr. Schreber's own writings, it is clear that he also used a "scientifically" elaborated system of relentless mental and corporeal pressure alternating with occasional indulgence, a methodical sequence of studiously applied terror interrupted by compensatory periods of seductive benevolence and combined with ritual observances that he as a reformer incorporated into his overall missionary scheme of physical education.

To return to the son's statement about his acclimatization "from youth to enduring both heat and cold," we learn from the father's textbook on child care that ". . . beginning about three months after birth the infant's skin should be cleaned by the use of cold ablutions *only*, for the purpose of physically toughening up the child from its earliest days." While it is advisable to administer warm baths to infants up to the age of six months, "one may then pass to cool and cold *general* ablutions which should be performed at least once daily and for which the body should be purposefully prepared by prior local applications of cold water" (italics in the original).

In an earlier volume entitled *Das Buch der Gesundheit* (The Book of Health), Dr. Schreber recommends that children's "eyelids, eyebrows, and temporal areas be treated daily with cold water," which in his view will make for sharper vision, and in a later text he instructs parents to wash the eyes of their babies thoroughly a number of times a day with a little sponge through the first several months of life.

This book also offers detailed advice on how to combat crying in young children:

. . . crying and whimpering without reason express nothing but a whim, a mood, and the first emergence of stubbornness; they must be dealt with positively, through quick distraction of attention, serious words, knocking on the bed (actions which usually startle the child and make him stop crying), or if all this be to no avail, through the administration of comparatively mild, intermittently repeated, corporeal admonishments. It is essential that this treatment be continued until its purpose is attained. . . . Such a procedure is necessary only once or, at most, twice—and then one is master of the child forever. From then on one glance, one word, one single menacing gesture are sufficient to rule the child. . . .

The whole problem of the "cry baby," of later moodiness and stubbornness in children can thus be settled, according to Dr. Schreber, during their first year of life. This is also the best time to train the young child "in the art of renouncing." The mode of training recommended here is simple and effective: while the child sits on the lap of its nurse or nanny, the latter eats and drinks whatever she desires; however intense the child's oral needs may become under such circumstances, they must never be gratified. Not a morsel of food must be given the child besides its regular three meals a day. The father is particularly strict in this situation. He relates an episode "in my own family" when a nurse, with one of the Schreber children sitting on her lap, was eating pears and could not resist the impulse to give a small piece of the pear to the begging child, though this had been strictly *verboten*. The nurse was immediately fired, and since news about this drastic action spread quickly among the children's nurses then available in Leipzig, the father writes, from then on he had "no further trouble with any other such erring maids or nurses."

In a different connection Dr. Schreber states: "Physical diseases in children . . . are decisive tests of the inner sense, true character tests." He then reports another incident from his family life:

One of my children had fallen ill at the age of one and a half and the only treatment, though a dangerous one, giving any hope for saving his life was possible only through the completely quiet submissiveness of the young patient. It succeeded, because the child had been accustomed from the beginning to the most absolute obedience toward me, whereas otherwise the child's life would in all probability have been beyond any chance of rescue.

The two episodes, the pear incident and the child's illness, seem to me particularly illuminating. They indicate that the strict rules set down in Dr. Schreber's writings, far from being theoretical educational concepts, were literally, meticulously, and often personally enforced in the upbringing of his own children. In other words, here we have samples of those actual and concrete experiences for which we have been searching in our effort to learn more about the childhood of the young Daniel Paul. It is quite possible, indeed, that the child in question who, already at the age of 1½, showed "the most absolute obedience" toward the father, was our patient himself. The gender used in the original German text (*"des* kleinen Patient*en"*) makes it clear that it was a male child. It may also have been the elder brother, of course. If so, the experiences of the younger brother cannot have been much different; for the father who so proudly announces to the world the lifesaving success of his educational system can hardly be expected to have refrained, in the case of the second son, from using measures closely resembling those which he believed had served him so well for the first.

I do not examine here the host of problems these practices pose with regard to their impact on the ego development of the child. Suffice it to say we shall presently encounter certain psychic derivatives of these experiences as components of some of the "miracled-up" delusional formations that fill the pages of the *Memoirs*.

One can assume that by the time the child Schreber entered his third or fourth year of life, he had already undergone a notable degree of traumatization. At about that time the father, bent as he was on his stated goal "to eradicate the child's crude nature . . . and to put down its ignoble parts," embarked on a more complex and more ambitious program of regimented upbringing. He brought to bear on the child the whole system of medical gymnastics, calisthenic exercises, orthopedic appliances, and other regulatory practices which he had invented and which are described in detail in preceding chapters of this book.

The young boy seems to have been subjected to what Sylvester has named "gadget experience," that is, a combination of ego-disruptive experiences that come from the application of mechanical contraptions on the child's body, for orthopedic or other purposes, and that can result in serious distortions of the child's body image, ego structure, reality testing, and object relations.

That the sometimes crippling effects of such early "gadget experience" did not fully materialize during Schreber's childhood—the sister's testimony, if correct, suggests a comparatively mild form of childhood neurosis—and were only later "miracled-up" during his psychotic illness, may be due to several circumstances. One of these may have been the fact that the father, with all his compulsive rigidity and authoritarian strictness, applied his mechanical contraptions and other methods of physical and mental restraint only inter-mittently, that is, for a number of hours during the day or night. Also, the effects of the father's alternating practices—periods of enforced passivity followed by intense physical activity—have to be considered. An illustration of this procedure will be presented below in connection with my discussion of Dr. Schreber's rules for the sitting child.

Another relevant factor appears to be connected with the father's psycho-pathology in a more direct way. His defensive struggle against his own sadism is frequently manifest in his texts on child care; for instance, he insists that all manipulatory practices and coercive actions on the child's body be performed "*iucunde*," that is, in a manner pleasurable and enjoy-able to the child. The impact of this procedure on the child's psychosexual development, the intense overstimulation thus produced, the premature inter-ference with libidinal needs in general, and the emphasis on the homosexual libido in particular, the peculiar mixture of once brutally enforced, then again pleasurably induced passivity—all these require little further analytic elaboration. Nor is it surprising to find among the elder Schreber's prescrip-tions such additional suggestions as his recommendation of enemas as "the most subtle form of laxative."

He is tireless in his campaign against masturbation, which necessitates "incessant vigilance" on the part of parents and educators, because it is "this insidious plague of youth . . . which makes the unfortunate [youngsters] stupid and dumb, fed up with life [*lebensmüde*], overly disposed to sickness, vulnerable to countless diseases of the lower abdomen and to diseases of the nervous system [*Nervenkrankheiten*], and very soon makes them impotent as well as sterile."

The son's version of these paternal threats and dire pronouncements forms an essential part of the *Memoirs*, even as their original German title indi-cates: *Denkwürdigkeiten eines Nervenkranken*. We may well be justified in recognizing in this title the reminiscences (or may we say confessions?) of one who saw himself sick and impotent as a result of masturbation long before his delusions took on a religious-mystical character. In the language of the medical report accompanying the *Memoirs:* "He thought he was dead and rotten, suffering from the plague, [with] all sorts of horrible manipula-tions being performed on his body. . . ." That Schreber believed masturba-tion had something to do with his illness is also shown by the label *Pestkranker* he applied to himself, thus employing the very term *Pest* (plague) that the father uses to characterize the plague of masturbation. The patient further reports: "At various times I had on my body fairly definite signs of the manifestations of plague."

Another factor of considerable import in Schreber's early life must have been the voice of the father, not merely in the usual sense as the guiding and directing voice of his childhood, but more specifically as the chief instrument of the father's multifold activities as fiery preacher and orator, indefatigable teacher, and emitter of verbal exhortations, injunctions, and blandishments. In his obituary, Politzer emphasizes the father's restless energy. From all we know, the elder Schreber, rather than being an ordinary physician and orthopedist, was really a reformer with a mission, an educator with a single goal, or, in the son's terminology, an "Apostle" and "God"—a verbose and talkative sort of "God," we may add. A note of relentless sermonizing runs through most of his books, and one can almost hear his voice with its long-winded sentences, admonishing, lecturing, scolding, and exhorting. An interesting question arises here: Was Schreber's choice of profession—law—influenced by these experiences or rather by the fact that the paternal grandfather had been a lawyer, or by both?

On the basis of our knowledge to date, it is not possible to answer this question. Reviewing this sketchy outline of the nature and extent of the paternal influences to which the young Schreber was exposed, it must also be noted that the data presented are open to various inferences. With regard to the authoritarian way of upbringing, the anti-masturbation campaign, the paternal harangues, the spirit of the times—der Zeitgeist—must be considered. With respect to the father, one might reason he was the type of "symbiotic father," whose all-pervasive presence, usurpation of the maternal role, and other domineering features (overtly sadistic as well as paternalistically benevolent, punitive as well as seductive) lent themselves to their fusion with the bizarre God hierarchy characteristic of the son's delusional system.

As to the significance of the collected data, it seems to me that our reconstructive approach based on these informational sources provides us with enough material to be included in an evaluation of Schreber's childhood experiences and that our exploration of such experiences throws light on the early traumatic relationship between father and son.

I therefore now propose to examine from a psychoanalytic angle one aspect of this relationship, the origin of the "divine miracles." I shall attempt to correlate the son's delusional productions with his actual childhood experiences at the hands of his father. I shall also demonstrate how they emerge as "miracled-up" during the psychotic illness and are projected in various chapters of the Memoirs, as if the pages of the manuscript that Schreber filled with his delusional descriptions had served him as a welcome screen for the externalization and concretization of his fantasies. (The word "miracled-up"—"angewundert" in the original—constantly used by Schreber in this connection is in a sense indicative of this mechanism; in part a neologism, the term not only suggests the startling appearance of something unexpected, but also the subject's act of externalizing this inner percept and then staring wonderingly at it as a miraculous, incomprehensible, and at the same time concrete phenomenon of the outer world.)

THE GENESIS OF THE "DIVINE MIRACLES"

In one of his last papers Freud writes about the genetic approach in psychoanalysis: "What we are in search of is a picture of the patient's forgotten years that shall be alike trustworthy and in all essential respects complete." He then advances the proposition that there is a kernel of historical truth in psychotic delusions, that "in them something that has been experienced in infancy and then forgotten re-emerges—something that the child has seen or heard at a time . . . and that now forces its way into consciousness." According to Freud, part of the analytic process "consists in liberating the fragment of historic truth from its distortions and its attachments to the actual present day and in leading it back to the point in the past to which it belongs." Waelder, later applying this concept to the clinical study of paranoia, sees the paranoid symptoms as a "return of the denied," and I have expanded these views with respect to certain auditory-tactile sensations experienced by the child during the first years of life.

This approach, then, first made by Freud, to the historical truth .(albeit distorted) in the mental productions of psychotic patients, would appear to contribute much to a fuller understanding of such productions. The "divine miracles" that abound in Schreber's *Memoirs* are a case in point. There are literally hundreds of these miracles scattered throughout its text, and Chapter XI, entitled "Bodily Integrity Damaged by Miracles," offers a detailed description of many of them. The opening paragraph of this chapter reads:

From the first beginnings of my contact with God up to the present day my body has continuously been the object of divine miracles. If I wanted to describe all these miracles in detail I could fill a whole book with them alone. I may say that *hardly a single limb or organ in my body escaped being temporarily damaged by miracles, nor a single muscle being pulled by miracles,* either moving or paralyzing it according to the respective purpose. Even now the miracles which I experience hourly are still of a nature as to frighten every other human being to death. . . . In the first year of my stay at Sonnenstein sanatorium the miracles were of such a threatening nature that I thought I had to fear almost incessantly for my life, my health or my reason. . . . [In a footnote Schreber adds:] This, as indeed the whole report about the miracles enacted on my body, will naturally sound extremely strange to all other human beings, and one may be inclined to see in it only the product of a pathologically vivid imagination. In reply, I can only give the assurance that *hardly any memory from my life is more certain* than the miracles recounted in this Chapter. *What can be more definite for a human being than what he has lived through and felt on his own body?* Small mistakes may have occurred as my anatomical knowledge is *naturally only that of a layman* . . . [italics added].

Thus, the patient's mode of experiencing his inner stimuli as being of out-side origin and the hypercathected quality of these experiences are stated with extraordinary sharpness.

A word is needed on Schreber's reference to himself as a layman. He does so throughout his book. I have found that whenever he mentions his status as a layman, he directly or indirectly alludes to his relation with his father, the physician and orthopedist, whose domain is human anatomy. The first sentence of the first chapter (entitled "God and Immortality") of the *Memoirs* contains the same apologetic statement "I as a layman" in matters of anatomy and health, as if the son dared but hesitatingly and fearfully enter the discussion of this subject, that is, the father's personal medical domain.

In fact, Chapter XI in its entirety deals with those changes in Schreber's own anatomy brought on by the miracles constantly performed on his body by God. The son enumerates a long list of such miracles beginning with the threatened removal of his genitals, proceeding to the removal of various inner organs, to the damages inflicted on his head, chest, abdomen, and nerves, and ending with the enactment of miracles on his muscles and skeleton, including his coccyx bone. In examining the nature of these miracles, the analyst once again is struck by the marked similarities between the miracles listed in the *Memoirs* and the physical manipulations experienced by Schreber at the hands of his father. Here are two examples reported by the son:

One of the most horrifying miracles was the so-called *compression-of-the-chest-miracle* which I endured. . . . It consisted in the whole chest wall being compressed, so that the state of oppression caused by the lack of breath was transmitted to my whole body. . . .

Next to the *compression-of-the-chest-miracle*, the most abominable of all miracles was the *head-being-tied-together-machine*[2] . . . which compressed my head as though in a vise by turning a kind of screw, causing my head temporarily to assume an elongated almost pear-shaped form. It had an extremely threatening effect, particularly as it was accompanied by severe pain. The screws were loosened temporarily but only very gradually, so that the compressed state usually continued for some time.

Superficially viewed, all this might appear to be a typical manifestation of the "influencing machine," which occurs in the persecutory delusions of many schizophrenics. However, closer examination of the available sources has convinced me that there is a realistic core in this delusional material. The historical truth about these two miracles can be found in the following paternal practices described in Dr. Schreber's books.

The father, obsessively preoccupied with the children's postural system,

[2] The German names of these two miracles—*das Engbrüstigkeitswunder* and *die Kopfzusammenschnürungsmaschine*—point almost directly to the "historical truth," that is, to the paternal manipulations. Especially the second term, *Kopfzusammenschnürungs-maschine*, graphically portrays the act of tying the head with a rope or belt.

invented a series of orthopedic apparatus, the so-called *Schreber'sche Gerade-halter* (see Figures 3–5, pp. 53–54), to secure a straight and upright body posture day or night. One of these contraptions consisted of a system of iron bars fastened to the chest of the child as well as to the table near which the child was sitting; the horizontal iron bar pressed against the chest and prevented any movement forward or sideward, giving only some freedom to move backward to an even more rigidly upright position. I believe that this device, apparently applied for several hours every day, constitutes the fragment of historic truth recognizable in the "compression-of-the-chest" delusion.

In order to ensure a proper growth of the skull, especially of the jaw, chin, and teeth, the father also constructed a helmetlike device (see Figure 6, p. 54), which by his own admission was apt to produce "a certain stiffening effect on the head" and should therefore be worn only one or two hours per day. I am inclined to regard this contraption as the historical forerunner of the son's delusional "head-being-tied-together-machine," which obviously caused him to complain that "the compressed state usually continued for some time" after its enforced use. To enhance the effect of the helmetlike *Kopf-halter* or to prevent any tilting of the head forward or sideward when the helmet contraption was not applied, the child had to wear leather belts tied by buckles around the head and shoulders for the entire day. It seems that this device in the son's delusional (perhaps not so delusional) elaboration was felt as compressing the "head as though in a vise by turning a kind of screw" and finally as producing "in the skull a deep cleft or rent roughly along the middle. . . ."

Another heavy belt was used at bedtime (see Figures 1 and 2, p. 52) to make sure that the child remained in a supine position all night long. This belt was fastened to the bed and ran tighly across the child's chest, thus keeping his body posture straight as well as supine through the night. This gadget may well have contributed to making the "compression-of-the-chest" miracle one of the most horrifying recorded by Schreber. It may also have been the nucleus of truth around which further delusional ideas developed, namely, the "tying-to-earth" or "tying-to-celestial-bodies" miracles occurring in the *Memoirs*. The tying of the patient's body to such "celestial bodies" expresses in the concretized language of the schizophrenic the thinglike quality as well as the projection of the unresolved libidinal ties with the deified father.

Schreber himself connected the heat and cold miracles discussed earlier with concrete events experienced in his childhood, that is, with his spartan upbringing. The genesis of other miracles is not always so clear and has to be reconstructed from the available material. In Chapter XI of the *Memoirs* we read, for example, that "my eyes and the muscles of the lids which serve to open and close them were an almost uninterrupted target for miracles." That the prescriptions of Schreber's father included a whole system of eye-washing, eye-sponging, lid-cleansing procedures and that this system was put into action several times a day beginning in the postnatal period, has already been mentioned. Katan interprets Schreber's description of the "miracled-up, cursorily made little men" dripping down on his head and eyes as symbolic of a nocturnal emission. This may well be so, if the phenomenon of the mysterious "little men" is viewed mainly from the standpoint of the genital libidinal organization. By displacement, the eye readily becomes a symbol of the genitals, male as well as female.

Evidently Schreber's delusions are the end products of complex mental processes into which instinctual drives, introjective-projective mechanisms, libidinal conflicts, regressive contributions from multiphasic sources, and restitution processes are fused to become a single entity, possibly in the manner of the Galtonian photographs, of which Lewin speaks in a different context. In my present approach, I chose to omit the investigation of those areas, significant though they may be, and to follow instead Freud's suggestion, that is, to focus attention on the demonstrable fragments of "historical truth" as one element in Schreber's delusional formations.

While the instinctual drives, therefore, are unquestionably basic to the formation of the phenomena which Schreber reports, these phenomena cannot be fully understood ontogenetically without taking into account the memory traces laid down by the paternal manipulations during infancy. Both father and son seem to be particularly interested in treatments administered to the eyes, the former *prescribing* more and more procedures to ensure their proper functioning, the latter *describing* more and more miracles performed on them. A comparison of the paternal and filial texts makes it difficult, at times, to know exactly where the father's medical mythology ends and the son's delusional mythology begins.

The father, for instance, aside from the ophthalmological prescriptions in his regular textbooks, devotes a supplementary booklet to *The Systematically Planned Sharpening of the Sense Organs*, in which he insists on all sorts of ocular exercises during childhood, such as quick distraction of visual attention, forcing "the child to focus on sharp objects, on detailed observation of little objects, on [visual] comparisons of these among themselves, on estimating distances, etc." In the son's "miracled-up" world, such early experiences seem to emerge in the following context (Chapter XI) :

Whenever I showed signs of being unwilling to allow my eye-lids to be pulled up and down and actually opposed it, the "little men" became annoyed and expressed this by calling me "wretch"; if I wiped them off my eyes with a sponge, it was considered by the rays as a sort of crime against God's gift of miracles. By the way, wiping them away had only a very temporary effect, because the "little men" were each time set down afresh [on the eyes].

Given the archaic language of the primary process, a clearer description of the later vicissitudes of those early eye manipulations can hardly be expected: the conflict-producing situation, the intense stimulation, the guilt, the masturbatory and homosexual libidinization of what must have been felt originally as attacks on the body integrity. Even the paternal sponge used in the daily eye-wash appears here. Nor are there omitted the father's statements that his manipulations are really of the greatest benefit for and a genuine blessing to the child, a "gift of miracles," any rebellion against which is considered by the rays (father) as a serious crime.

In a later passage (Chapter XVIII), Schreber complains about his father's practices of forcefully distracting his visual attention and directing him to observe little objects:

As often as an insect . . . appears, a miracle *directs the movements of my eyes.*
I have not mentioned this miracle before, but it has been regularly enacted for years. Rays [father], after all, want constantly to see what pleases them. . . .
My eye muscles are therefore influenced to move in that direction toward which my glance *must* fall on things just created or else on a female being. . . .
(Italics in the original.)

In a footnote, Schreber adds that "miracles direct my gaze (turn my eyes) to the desired object."

To much of this delusional material Waelder's formulations of "noisy counterclaims" and of the "return of the denied" are applicable. The conflict-producing, scoptophilic impulse aimed at instinctual gratification—Schreber discusses his looking at insects, things just "created" or to be created, and so on, in the context of copulation, the sight of females, and voluptuousness—is warded off through denial and expressed through the counterclaim: "Rays want constantly to see what pleases them . . . ," that is, foremost a female being. In the "return of the denied" the instinctual impulse reappears in connection with "the desired object," while utilizing the "historical truth," namely, that originally the father had instructed the son to look, to observe, to follow the movements of objects with his eyes, and the like.

To turn to other aspects of the "divine miracles," it is noteworthy that the father's more voluminous writings, especially those which had an enormous popular appeal at the time of publication and passed through numerous subsequent editions, are replete with anatomical material. Almost one third of the *Buch der Gesundheit* is devoted to human anatomy. It contains 34 anatomical pictures, several of them full-page and in color. These pictures show the human figure *in toto* or in segments, now portions of the viscera and abdomen, now dissected parts of the skull, brain, skeleton, or the like. (See Figures 8 and 9, p. 55.)

The books *Kallipaedie, Medical Indoor Gymnastics, Pangymnastikon,* and *Anthropos* contain hundreds of anatomical illustrations showing the human figure in seemingly endless variety of positions and physical exercises. It is of special interest that most of this anatomical material is composed of male figures without a trace of genitals; a few isolated illustrations in those short book sections that deal with the secretory and urinary functions of the organism show the genitals, viewed not *in toto*, but rather as dissected, separate parts of the human anatomy.

The disruptive impact of all this on the young Schreber's body image is "miracled-up" in Chapter XI. It reads like a highly condensed, symbolized, archaically distorted, yet essentially correct version of many of the paternal physical maneuvers to which the young Schreber was subjected, a sort of "primary-process" catalogue of those remote infantile experiences, shaped, altered, and strongly cathected ("deified") by the father-son conflict. In this sense, Chapter XI can be understood as an archaic textbook of the father's as well as Schreber's own anatomy: gullet and lungs, pharynx and stomach, abdomen and intestines, muscles and bones are "pictured" just as methodically, if delusionally, as they are in the father's anatomical texts and illustrations. The "picturing of human beings" is mentioned in this chapter as well as in other parts of the *Memoirs*, though in contrast to the father's works, unaccompanied by illustrations. (We know, however, from the case histories discovered by Baumeyer, that Schreber used to draw human figures during the years of his confinement in the insane asylum.) These findings lend strong support to Katan's views that the father not only represents the boy's ideal of masculinity, but also that the God who persecuted Schreber represented part of Schreber himself and that God's genitals represented Schreber's genitals.

The impairment of the body image is further "miracled-up" in the delusional reduction of Schreber's height. One of the miracles caused "a change in my whole stature (diminution of body size)," he writes. Mittelmann has pointed to the serious impairment of the body image as a result of motor restriction in childhood. Greenacre finds that such subjective sensations of changed total body size or of the size of certain body parts occur in individuals who at critical periods in early life have been "subject to external stresses of a nature which upset the integrity of the self-perception." The presence of such external stresses in Schreber's childhood has been amply documented. It is likely that the reduction of the son's body size is another expression of identification with the father's small body. I am inclined to view, partly in accordance with Katan, the "little men" as representing Schreber's homosexual objects, modeled on the father's body, which appears "miracled-up" in the hundreds of anatomical "little-men" illustrations mentioned above.

The connections between the father's actual handling or observing the child and the "miracles" later enacted on the adult patient are lucidly stated in Schreber's description of the "miracles" performed on his muscles and skeleton. In his wording: "All my muscles were and are, still today, miracled around[3] in order to hinder all my movements or to prevent any activity which

[3] The original German for "miracled around," *herumgewundert*, carries the connotation of *herummachen* or *hantieren*, that is, "manipulated."

I am about to perform." Here the effects of the father's interference with the child's motor activities are indicated.

In "miracling-up" these events, Schreber notes that attempts are made at "paralyzing my fingers when I play the piano or write, and at damaging my kneecap to the point of destroying my capacity to march, when I walk around in the garden or in the corridor." As to the attack on Schreber's capacity to march—in the original German, *Marschfähigkeit*—I found evidence in the father's writings that cufflike braces may have been applied to the child's legs to prevent the development of bowed legs. (See Figure 10.)

Among the various miracles directed against his bones, Schreber lists those which resulted in his "skull [being] repeatedly sawn asunder . . . and partly pulverized" (through the action of the "head-being-tied-together-machine"?) and in damage to his ribs (caused by the "compression-of-the-chest-machine"?). Ultimately, these are variations of the castration theme that he

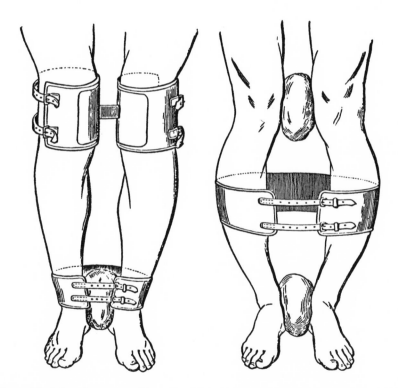

Figure 10 / Iron braces used to prevent or correct bowed leg deformity (reproduced from Dr. Schreber's printed works).

mentions first. This part of his story culminates in the description of the "coccyx-miracle":

Its purpose was to make sitting or even lying down impossible. I was not allowed to remain for long in one and the same position or at the same occupation; when I was walking, they attempted to make me lie down, only to chase me promptly from my reclining position when I was lying down. The rays seemed to lack any understanding of the fact that a human being, since he really exists, *must be somewhere.* . . . I had become an unwelcome person for the rays [God], in whatever position or posture I would find myself or whatever activity I would engage in [italics in the original].

I now compare this account of the coccyx-miracle with certain rules laid down by the father for the child's postural system. After explaining the proper mode of sitting during childhood, that is, straight and upright at all times, Dr. Schreber insists that the act of sitting down be carried out *gleichseitig*, that is, on both buttocks simultaneously. He warns parents and educators alike that the child's tendency to sit down *ungleich* (unevenly) has to be fought against because of its harmful effects on the spinal column. He continues:

. . . one must see to it that children always sit straight and on both buttocks simultaneously . . . neither first on the right nor first on the left side. . . . As soon as they begin to lean back, it is time to change their sitting position to an absolutely still, supine one. . . . It is important to train children of this age [from 2 to 7] to acquire absolutely straight posture and movements, because it is more difficult to achieve this at a later age. When children are tired, they should be made to lie down. But if they are up and around, they should be forced to hold themselves erect in walking, standing, playing, and in all their activities. This can best be done by insisting that as soon as a child behaves in a relaxed or lazy way, he is made to lie down, if only for a few moments [as a punishment].

Of interest in this reconstructive approach to Schreber's early history are the vicissitudes of the castration threat that he experienced as a young boy. To paraphrase Hartmann and Kris, one may say with regard to the Schreber home: there was always castration in the air. The father's aggressive and coercive actions; the orthopedic contraptions; the disrupted, dismembered, and dissected aspects of the human body; the violence and authoritarian impetus of the injunctions; the sequence masturbation-plague-sterility-insanity (castration)—all belong in this setting. As to the castrative aspects prevailing in Schreber's early life situation, I came upon evidence that such threats were limited not merely to their appearance in word and picture. They were part, so to speak, of the boy's actual environment from the age of 2.

In 1844, the father became the owner and director of the orthopedic institute in Leipzig. Under Dr. Schreber's management the institute soon grew into a well-known *Heilanstalt* (sanatorium), which was repeatedly enlarged and to which orthopedic patients from many countries flocked. Ritter reports that these crippled and mutilated people mingled freely with the Schreber children, joined them in the garden of the institute, took part in their games, and so on. These early experiences in the orthopedic *Heilanstalt*, together with their castration aspects, must have been connected with and then blended into the patient's later experiences in the *Nervenheilanstalt* (psychiatric hospital) where he expected "unmanning," was in fear of being put to death, saw himself "dead and rotten," and felt that he was suffering from general paralysis. The last-mentioned condition is said to have played a role in the brother's death in 1877.

It is likely that among the inmates of Dr. Schreber's *Heilanstalt* during those early years of our patient's life there were at least some who, superficially viewed, resembled certain paretics, paraplegics, catatonics, and so on, in the Sonnenstein sanatorium half a century later. Schreber's confusion with respect to this situation is recorded in his case history. Also his expectation, immediately on entering the asylum, of being tortured, manhandled, and mutilated is probably overdetermined as well as "concretized" through his childhood contacts with amputees and otherwise physically damaged people in the father's orthopedic institute. A similar "concretizing" element may have played a part with regard to the paternal predictions of impotence and sterility resulting from masturbation. The lack of offspring in Schreber's marriage may well have been experienced as the verification, inexorable and ominous, of the father's dire predictions and may thus have become an important factor in precipitating the illness.

A miracle not mentioned in Chapter XI, but frequently occurring in the case history, is the "bellowing miracle." Whether its kernel of truth is based on the father's activities as a lecturer and orator, on his sermonizing, haranguing, and other vocal pursuits (the father even prescribes "systematic, constantly repeated [verbal] admonishments" to combat poor pronunciation of words or syllables by children), I am not prepared to say. That there exists a direct connection between the father and the "bellowing miracle" is shown by the occurrence of the latter in relation to the sun: Schreber bellowed and shouted at the sun. At one time two suns appeared in the sky—an allusion to both father and elder brother. My assumption that the latter played a role in the delusion of the two suns is supported by Schreber's statement that the other sun was derived from the Cassiopeia group of stars (Chapter VI). In the preceding chapter he speaks of the "Brothers of Cassiopeia."

Another enigma, I suggest, can be made intelligible through an inquiry into its "historical truth." At one point during his illness Schreber thought of himself as being dead and decomposing. At the same time, he fantasied that a newspaper containing his own obituary notice had been put into his hands. Since, undoubtedly, no such report existed, we must ask ourselves—in order to arrive at the truth (albeit distorted)—whose obituary actually *was* published and *was* read by the Schreber family at the time of *whose* death?

This delusion must refer to the death notices in the papers of the father and probably also the brother. As I mentioned previously, the father died of acute ileus on November 10, 1861, after a brief hospitalization of a day or two. More than three decades later, the son tells us that precisely "on November 8 or 9th, my illness began to assume a menacing character . . . the following day we travelled [from Dresden] to Leipzig, direct to Professor Flechsig at the University Clinic. . . ." That same night of November 10[4] or 11, 1893, the sick son made the first suicide attempt, had himself hospitalized in Leipzig, and felt that he was dead (the father had died in a Leipzig hospital). There he made another suicide attempt a few days later, and soon began to believe that he was suffering, among other symptoms, from ileus—the very disease to which the father had succumbed.

The details of these events can be found in Chapter IV of the *Memoirs*. It is perhaps not surprising to note that all three of Schreber's hospitalizations, though widely separated in years, took place during the month of November. He also gives this month of a later year, 1895, as the date on which the connection between his emasculation and redeemer ideas was established, and he began to reconcile himself to the former. These anniversary reactions are noteworthy phenomena in Schreber's case in that they span a period of several decades.

[4] At that time some Leipzig newspapers had erroneously reported November 11, 1861, as the day of the father's death. Even this uncertainty seems to be reflected in the son's description of his own hospitalization, 32 years later. His otherwise very detailed report in the *Memoirs* (Chapter IV) does not make it clear whether he was hospitalized on November 10 or 11, 1893.

10 / Analysis of a Delusion: "Margraves of Tuscany and Tasmania"[1]

In this section I shall attempt to demonstrate that one of Schreber's delusions, besides dealing with the infantile father-son conflict, reflects elements of his unresolved relationship with his mother, whose personality and/or influence have otherwise remained conspicuously absent from the *Memoirs*.

The known facts about Schreber's adulthood—that he became the presiding judge of the Saxonian Superior Court, was married for a number of years, and ran for an important political office—make it appear likely that before his breakdown he must have attained a measure of adequate ego functioning and may also have reached or at least approximated the state of genital organization. Freud has brilliantly elucidated the dynamics and vicissitudes of Schreber's inverted oedipal relation to his father. Thus we may legitimately ask: Where is Schreber's positive oedipus complex? Where in the autobiographical *Memoirs* are its precipitates or vestiges? Though it is hazardous to try to reconstruct this phase of Schreber's life on the basis of a single delusional utterance, I am inclined to assume that his oedipal problem finds expression in the fantasy that the Schrebers, who belonged to "the highest aristocracy of Heaven," bore the title of "Margraves of Tuscany and Tasmania."

Freud connects this fantasy with the frustration Schreber suffered in his marriage. "It brought him no children," Freud writes, "his family line threatened to die out, and it seems that he felt no little pride in his birth and lineage." Here, incidentally, lies another kernel of historical truth; one of Schreber's ancestors, the physician and botanist Johann Christian Daniel von Schreber (1739–1810), was knighted in 1791. Baumeyer mentions that his coworker, Ayem, believes that this fantasy may be connected with the medieval event of Canossa.

Nonetheless, this still leaves unanswered the question of the origin of the delusional title "Margraves of Tuscany and Tasmania." Of course, one may be tempted to dismiss the fantasy with a reference to its obvious clang association. Apart from the fact that Schreber's recorded clang associations are of a more direct nature and appear in a very different setting (usually as

[1] This essay appeared originally as part of "The Miracled-up World of Schreber's Childhood," 1959.

isolated, bisectional formations, for example, "Santiago-Carthago"), his choice of such specific geographic-historical areas as Tuscany and Tasmania, presided over and owned by the Schreber nobility, invites investigation. Moreover, the circumstance that this delusion concerns Schreber's family and not his body (as do many of his other fantasies) arouses our interest.

In expanding Freud's and Baumeyer's notions and inquiring more closely into the content of the delusion, I have come to understand it as a delusionally distorted derivative of the "miracled-up" vestiges of Schreber's lost oedipus complex. Since such vestiges must be derived from the original oedipal constellation, their analysis may provide us with information on Schreber's oedipus complex.[2]

At this point, a somewhat lengthy historical detour becomes necessary. It is important for the English-speaking reader to realize that the episode of Canossa, though belonging to medieval history, stood at the center of a furious political battle called *Kulturkampf*. Essentially a struggle between the Protestants and the Catholics for political and cultural supremacy in the newly unified German Reich, it dominated the domestic scene during the 1870s and 1880s. Schreber's candidature for the *Reichstag* falls into this period. Also, part of his cosmology—with its multiple references to Catholicism and Protestantism, to the Jesuits and the Pope, to his fear that the Catholics would take over Protestant Saxony and subsequently the planets, solar system, and universe—is linked up in Schreber's mind with the *Kulturkampf*. The political personalities that Schreber mentions by name in the early chapters of the *Memoirs*, such as Bismarck and the Pope, the Cardinals Rampolla and Galimberti, were protagonists in that heated controversy. Chapters V through VII are incomprehensible unless these facts are taken into account.

According to Schreber, the "Catholicizing of Saxony and Leipzig" was imminent. The intensity of his conflict is revealed in the asylum material that tells of Schreber's own plans to convert to Catholicism. Thus, since he took an active part in politics and was a candidate for election to Parliament in 1884, the year he fell ill for the first time, he found himself in the midst of a major emotional and political crisis. An essential aspect of his conflict was that *running for the Reichstag meant running against Bismarck*, the most powerful father figure then in Germany, who all his life was sternly opposed to parliamentary (that is, filial) intrusion. Another factor aggravating Schreber's difficulties must be related to the circumstance that at the very time he saw himself, his family, and his country endangered by the spread of Catholicism, the reigning king of Saxony actually was a Catholic.

---

[2] Katan, exploring the patient's prepsychotic phase, focuses attention on the loss of the positive oedipus complex in schizophrenic illness, a loss that results in a marked reinforcement of the pregenital fixations, weakens contact with reality, and increases the state of narcissism. These findings throw further light on Schreber's choice of the megalomanic title.

As one studies the early chapters of the *Memoirs,* one finds them filled with archaic descriptions of the *Kulturkampf* situation. This is hardly surprising because just before falling ill, Schreber had lived through the whole controversy. His personal participation in the struggle (the *Reichstag* candidacy) had obviously reactivated his own unconscious conflicts, giving rise to delusional elaboration of the events, the naming of some of the chief protagonists, etc. To return to the delusional title "Margraves of Tuscany and Tasmania": Why this particular combination?

The second part of the fantasy, Tasmania, does not present very much difficulty. As every student of colonial history knows, the island of Tasmania was originally a British penal colony. Schreber, a prominent jurist versed in law as well as history, must almost certainly have known this. The question of sending convicts to remote areas overseas was widely discussed in Europe, and Tasmania was known as the "jail of the Empire" during the mid-nineteenth century. To the public mind such penal colonies with their population of criminals were places of horror, of which an old chronicler said: *"Hic homines patricidae habitant"* (Here live men, murderers of their fathers). In all likelihood then, Schreber's choice of Tasmania signifies prison and punishment.

This assumption receives support from the analysis of a parapraxia appearing in another of Schreber's delusions. In enumerating the various *Kulturkampf* figures, Schreber lists the above-mentioned Catholic dignitaries as "Cardinals Rampolla, Galimberti, and Casati. . . ." So far as I could ascertain, there was no Cardinal Casati. The only person of that name, a contemporary of the two prelates and also of Schreber, was the explorer and geographer Gaetano Casati (1838–1902), who for a time joined the African expeditions of Emin Pasha and later of Stanley. While serving under Emin Pasha, he was taken prisoner by the natives, tied naked to a tree, and tortured. Left to his fate, he managed to escape and later published an account of his and Emin Pasha's adventures, *Dieci Anni in Equatoria,* which was translated into German in 1891.

Schreber knew Italian quite well and wrote letters in Italian at Sonnenstein sanatorium (Baumeyer). Some of Schreber's descriptions about strange travels ("I traversed the earth from Lake Ladoga[3] to Brazil"), about the outbreak of devastating epidemics, and so on, resemble—shorn of their massive delusional distortions—the accounts of Casati's and Emin's African

[3] Emin Pasha's first expedition started from Lado, a region west of the upper Nile adjoining Lake Albert. In 1878, he became governor of the Equatorial Province and made his headquarters at Lado, where he was joined by Casati. In 1885, Emin Pasha and Casati were driven out of Lado by the Mahdist revolution and encountered serious difficulties with the authorities, hostile natives, dangers from epidemics, and so on. Lake Ladoga is, of course, situated between Finland and Russia, which Dr. Schreber "traversed" in his young years as the personal physician of a Russian aristocrat; Dr. Schnitzer also began his medical career as the personal physician of a nobleman, the Turkish governor of Dalmatia, with whom he traveled through parts of the Ottoman empire.

exploits. These reports, one may speculate, became fused with Schreber's reminiscences of stories related by his father concerning the latter's early travels in Russia and other countries. Though I cannot prove that Schreber read Casati's book (perhaps during his stay at the asylum), it is practically certain that he knew about the harrowing experiences of Emin Pasha and Casati, since the former—originally a physician of German-Jewish extraction by the name of Eduard Schnitzer—became a sensation in the Germany of those days because of his colorful career, fame, travels, and tireless efforts aimed at reform.

In this respect, Dr. Schnitzer–Emin Pasha was not unlike Dr. Schreber, our patient's father, and Casati, Emin's assistant, not unlike the patient himself. Both Casati and Schreber *fils* were the sons of physicians. Both were imprisoned and tortured, the one in the African jungle, the other—according to his own thinking—in the Sonnenstein sanatorium. There exist, however, more parallels between the two older men, Emin Pasha and Schreber's father. They both came from the eastern parts of Germany, both were graduated in medicine at approximately the same age, both went abroad shortly after their graduation, the former to Turkey and the latter to Russia. In 1858 or 1859, about three years before his death, Dr. Schreber suffered a serious head injury, possibly a skull fracture, from an iron ladder that fell on his head. In 1889, three years before his death, Emin Pasha met with an almost fatal accident, which caused the fracture of his skull. He was murdered in Africa in 1892.

All these facts were undoubtedly known to Schreber. The delusional fusion of Dr. Schnitzer (Emin Pasha) with Dr. Schreber (father, God), as hypothesized here, would explain to an extent Schreber's allusions to his persecution by Jews, baptized Jews, and Slavophiles. Emin Pasha was a baptized German Jew from Silesia, originally a Slavic province. Admittedly stretching a point somewhat, it is not unthinkable that Emin Pasha's sudden and violent death in 1892 had its repercussions on Schreber's precarious condition at that time. Emin Pasha's murder, occurring during Schreber's prepsychotic phase, could have reactivated Schreber's unconscious conflicts regarding his own oedipal crime. Instead of being exiled as a *convict* to Tasmania for having killed the father, he was made *presiding judge* in October, 1893. A month later he landed in his own "Tasmania," that is, in the mental hospital.

If Tasmania means punishment, it seems permissible to regard Tuscany as signifying crime. Historical Tuscany with its capital Florence has frequently had the same reputation as that attributed in biblical times to Sodom and Gomorrah, Nineveh, and so on—that is, places of sin, strife, incest, and homosexuality. Schreber's single statement about the "Margraves of Tuscany and Tasmania" characteristically occurs in the midst of a lengthy discourse on "soul murder" and on "a battle arising out of jealousy between souls already departed from life." The connection between "soul murder" and homosexuality has been demonstrated by Freud. With respect to the "battle arising out of jealousy," we have to return to Schreber's emotional state during the *Kulturkampf*.

The violent crisis in Germany had revived strong feelings about that earlier episode which in a similar struggle between the secular powers represented by the Emperor and the religious forces represented by the Pope had culminated in the Emperor's utter humiliation and defeat at Canossa in Tuscany in 1077 A.D. There are few moments in German history that have impressed later generations as intensely as the spectacle of Henry IV, the Emperor, standing in the courtyard of Canossa as a suppliant before Pope Gregory VII and Mathilde, Marchioness of Tuscany, Mistress of the castle of Canossa and then the most powerful lady in Europe. In fact, the defeat of the Emperor had been brought about by the alliance between the Pope and Mathilde of Tuscany. The Pope was accused of having intimate relations with Mathilde. Bismarck, in a famous speech before the Reichstag in 1872, revived the episode of Canossa when he exclaimed: "*Nach Canossa gehen wir nicht*" (To Canossa we shall not go), thus giving rise to what some historians have called the *furor protestanticus* in the Protestant German circles to which the Schreber family belonged.

The evidence that certain aspects of the Canossa story became part of Schreber's delusional system is based on various remarks contained in the *Memoirs*. I shall analyze here only the statement in Chapter VII, that "after the death of the present Pope and of an interim-Pope[4] Honorius, a further conclave could not be held. . . ." Since there is but one interim- or anti-Pope Honorius in the history of the papacy, this can refer only to the anti-Pope Honorius II (1061–1071) whose successor Gregory VII was the victor of Canossa. Thus "after the death of the present Pope" must refer to Honorius's predecessor, Pope Nicholas, who died in 1061 (Schreber's father died in 1861), and the naming of the interim-Pope Honorius must mean the "interregnum" of Schreber's brother Gustav, which came into being "after the death of the present Pope," that is, after the death of Schreber's father in 1861. The event of Canossa took place in 1077 (Schreber's brother died in 1877). The year 1877, then, marks the end of the brother's "interregnum," and Schreber was now in line to become the male head of the family. If my previous interpretation of the sequence "Cardinals Rampolla, Galimberti, Casati" is valid, the same chronology holds true in this statement. Rampolla and Galimberti, then Papal Secretary of State and Apostolic Legate respectively, represent Schreber's father and brother, while Casati who was tied to the tree is the patient himself.

His precarious state is indicated by his remark: "A further conclave could

---

[4] Schreber uses the expression *Zwischenpapst*, which clearly denotes the interim quality or interregnum character of this reign—an unmistakable allusion to the brother's "interregnum" after the father's death. By using the term *Zwischenpapst*, Schreber places a stamp of dubious, transient quality on the brother's "reign."

not be held because Catholics had lost their faith." The intensity of Schreber's conflict is revealed by this projection of his uncertainty and perplexity onto the Catholics, possibly also by his marriage in 1878, which followed the brother's suicide with conspicuous speed. Schreber could not accept the active masculine role, 1877, because such a role would have made him not merely the brother's successor, but also the usurper of the father's position; or, in terms of Canossa, 1077, he would have become Honorius's successor Gregory, the *triumphator* over the Emperor (father) and supposed lover of Mathilde (mother).

The sequence of events tends to corroborate this. When Schreber is called upon to assume the "presidency" in his family setting, he is unable to do so. Having been defeated in his candidacy for election to parliament, he falls ill for the first time. Promoted to the presidency of a high court almost a decade later, he again feels threatened and breaks down the second time. The threat of becoming a father himself, and in his own right, drives him back into the libidinized subjugation to the deified father of his early child-hood.

Nor does the Canossa story end here. Two dramatic episodes soon followed. First the Emperor's eldest son, Konrad, rebelled against his father, waged war against him, and had himself crowned king. Several years after Konrad's death the Emperor's second son, Henry (like our patient, his father's name-sake and second son!), revolted against the father who was taken prisoner by the son and forced to abdicate. Both sons' rebellions were actively sup-ported by Marchioness Mathilde of Tuscany. Also involved was the Emperor's wife Praxedis whom the Emperor suspected of having engaged in an illicit love affair with his son Konrad. The Empress openly admitted that she had committed adultery, but only at the behest of her husband, the Emperor. Historians disagree on the veracity of the accusations but hold that all these machinations, then publicly discussed and repeatedly negotiated before the *Reichstag*, contributed to the downfall of the Emperor.

Whether Schreber was familiar with all the details of the Canossa story is hard to say. As a jurist and student of history he probably was an avid and thorough reader, accustomed in his studies to going back to prime sources. Later, during "sleepless nights in the cell [of the asylum]," he tells us, "I produced my historical and geographical knowledge. . . ." It can be said with certainty, however, that Schreber knew about Canossa at least as much as the average German high-school student in that generation knew—and that in-cluded most of the essential events, their protagonists, dates, and the un-restrained passions connected with them. To the analytic observer the emo-tional impact of the Canossa affair is clear. Its implications and aftermath contain the dynamic aspects of a highly involved oedipal constellation.

In view of Schreber's excellent memory enhanced by the schizophrenic's hypermnesia for names and dates, in view also of the availability of with-drawn object cathexes for reinvestment in his restitution attempts aimed at regaining the lost objects via word representations, a full inquiry into such verbal formations as the "Margraves of Tuscany and Tasmania" appeared to me of some importance. Since in schizophrenia words and verbal ideas assume the role of objects, the analytic evaluation of these formations can supply us with information concerning the wishes, strivings, and conflicts attached to them. In the case under consideration, Schreber's choice of the delusional title with its particular names and historical-personal connotations seems to contain those vestigial elements of the "battle arising out of jealousy" in which past and present, history and individual fate, oedipal and pre-oedipal components coalesce. If my decoding of these elements is correct, the vestiges of Schreber's oedipus complex that are concretized, as it were, in the enigmatic title, can be understood in this way:

Margraves: the rebellious sons who in alliance with the powerful Marchioness
    (mother) humiliate and overthrow the father
Tuscany: the scene of the father's utter humiliation and defeat
Tasmania: the place of punishment for the oedipal crime

The climate of the times has always been an influential force in determining the contents of delusional ideation. The *Kulturkampf* situation in Schreber's Germany was such a force. The florid narcissism expressed in the self-aggrandizing title attached itself to great historical events which held a specific meaning for Schreber, that is, the vestiges of his lost positive Oedipus complex.

11 / Further Data on the "Historical Truth" in Schreber's Delusions [1]

In this paper I shall present further material and documentary evidence pertaining to the "historical truth" in Schreber's psychotic productions. In doing so I am aware that the method of presenting and using findings collected from outside sources, and not from the patient himself, differs from the accepted analytic method of gaining access to such data, which in analysis, of course, originate from one source alone, that is, the adult patient. In both applied and child analysis this is not the case. Likewise, during psychotic episodes in the treatment of adult patients, the method of gaining access to important material may legitimately change.

I therefore hold that the procedure I followed in my search for source material on Schreber—the systematic collection and analytic evaluation of authentic data derived from *all available sources*—is both permissible and useful, not merely because it corresponds to the approach chosen by many predecessors, but also because it enables us to correlate certain pathogenic events in Schreber's early life with some of his bizarre delusional formations in adulthood and thus to demonstrate what Freud has called the "historical truth" in a number of these heretofore unintelligible phenomena.

The analytic study of some of the patient's more conspicuous delusions reveals an unmistakable relation to his father's child-rearing practices, as exemplified by the otherwise incomprehensible *Kopfzusammenschnürungs-maschine* and *Steisswunder* ("head-being-tied-together-machine" and "coccyx-miracle"). I think we are justified in assuming, therefore, that the origin of these Schreberian productions is to be found in the early traumatic father-son relationship. In fact, one has only to drop the word *maschine* in the first neologism, that is, *Kopfzusammenschnürungsmaschine*, in order to arrive at the realistic core of its meaning in the patient's actual childhood experience, when the father contrived and applied a helmetlike tying device called a *Kopfhalter* ("head holder") to the child's head. Or, to understand the origin and meaning of the "coccyx miracle," one has but to compare the respective passages in the writings of father and son.

Such comparative observations can be helpful in clarifying other obscure

[1] This is an abbreviated and amended version of my article that appeared originally in the *International Journal of Psycho-Analysis*, Vol. 44 (1963), Pt. 2.

phenomena emerging during Schreber's illness. Another case in point is his frequent reference to those mysterious "little men," who have been the subject of much discussion in the literature.[2] Several of Dr. Schreber's books are filled with drawings and sketches of little human figures in a variety of physical poses, gymnastic exercises, calisthenics, and so on. That these figures represent in all likelihood the realistic precursors of the delusional "little men" can be seen from the specific wording used by the patient whenever he refers to them and their puzzling appearance. He calls them *hingemachte kleine Männer*, that is, men made or drawn (in the sense of produced), thus employing terms that point to their anal-sadistic derivation in his own thinking and their relation to the bewildering little men-figures in the father's literary productions.

Other delusional formations reported by Schreber, such as at times being without a stomach ("I existed frequently without a stomach"), having his "gullet and intestines . . . torn and made to vanish" and his skull sawn asunder and perforated, also appear to be connected with certain anatomical illustrations in the father's medical books.[3] These were published or reprinted during the years following the patient's birth. Schreber must certainly have seen them in manuscript or book form in early childhood and could have been overawed by the sight of vivid illustrations of dissected bodies and body parts. Since the father's anatomical volumes were abundantly and colorfully illustrated, they must have acquired for Schreber the emotionally charged meaning which picture books and illustrated fairy tales generally hold for children. In this situation, however, the very copiousness of the dissected body material over which the father as physician and orthopedist presided, may have lent itself to a fusion with the body-building and body-coercing paternal practices *in concretu*, thus adding to the ever-present castration threat in the early Schreber home.

The family lived in a wing of an orthopedic-surgical *Heilanstalt* (sanatorium) for deformed patients. It can be supposed that such an environment contributed to the elaboration of florid castration and sado-masochistic fantasies in a setting of active orthopedic-gymnastic practice.

The illustration (Figure 11) from Dr. Schreber's *Pangymnastikon* suggests the probable derivation of another "miracle" in the *Memoirs*, Schreber's puzzling *Mehrköpfigkeit* (multiple-headedness). In Chapter VI the patient reports:

. . . there was a time when souls in nerve-contact with me spoke of a *multiple-headedness* . . . which they encountered in me and from which they shrank in alarm, crying "For heaven's sake—that is *a human being with multiple heads*." I am fully aware how fantastic all this must sound to other people; and I therefore do not go so far as to assert that all I have recounted was objective

[2] I am indebted to Dr. Robert C. Bak who was the first to draw my attention to their connection with the numerous drawings in the father's *Ärztliche Zimmergymnastik*.

[3] See Figures 8 and 9, p. 55.

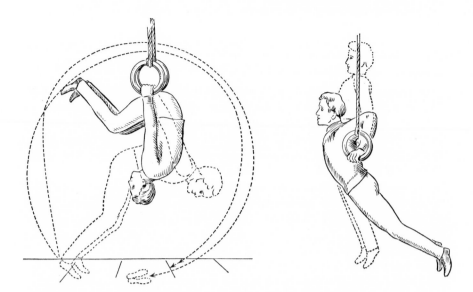

Figure 11 / "Little men" having "multiple heads" (reproduced from Dr. Schreber's *Pangymnastikon*).

reality; *I only relate the impressions retained as recollections in my memory.* (Italics added.)

One of many such, the illustration portrays heads coming out of one body in the fashion indicated by the patient. His statement about "impressions retained as recollections" also suggests a measure of subjective awareness as to the possible origin of his delusional fantasies. Be that as it may, the findings seem to demonstrate Schreber's early childhood experiences not only as the "kernel of truth" of some of his later delusions, but also as the core of the psychotic material "miracled-up" by the patient during his illness.

In his restitution efforts he attempted with the help of such experiences to regain the lost objects and to reestablish his unresolved infantile ties with them. One of the main features of this attempt at restitution consists, as Freud has shown, in reinforcing the cathexis of verbal and nonverbal representations. Hence the plethora of names and dates in Schreber's productions, especially the multitude and deification of the names representing the father; hence also the great number of "divine miracle" formations, their frequent repetition, neologistic naming, and detailed description in a steady flow of verbal material and delusional imagery.

These correlations furnish a glimpse into the patient's early life. Schreber was not unlike other psychotics who rarely, if ever, furnish sufficient evidence as to their developmental years and early family relations. Freud, to be sure, in analyzing the *Memoirs*, soon discovered "the shadowy sketch of infantile material" in them, and left to us latter-day analysts the task of filling in the gaps and supplying additional data for a fuller understanding of the case history.

In pursuance of this task, I present some new, well-substantiated information concerning Schreber's mother, about whom nothing was known until very recently and who is the subject of a valuable analytic study by White.[4] In the course of my search for authentic background material on the Schreber family, I secured a letter written by the patient's eldest sister, Anna, in 1909—two years before Schreber's death. It contains the following remarks about her parents: "Father discussed with our mother everything and anything; she took part in all his ideas, plans, and projects; she read the galley proofs of his writings with him, and was his faithful, close companion in everything."

It is understandable that a loyal daughter would tend to depict the parental relationship in harmonious fashion after the lapse of so many years (the father had died in 1861, the mother in 1907). The statement that both parents had worked in close collaboration on the paternal manuscripts—that is, on the very writings that are replete with the minute prescriptions, orthopedic procedures, and anatomical drawings later transmuted by the patient into the raw material for the "divine miracles"—led me to reflect on the likelihood that the mother must have been perceived by the patient as the willing and active participant in the paternal practices, manipulations, and coercive procedures. It thus becomes likely that the peculiar complexities of Schreber's deity, the central figure of the *Memoirs*, with the division into anterior and posterior "forecourts," upper and lower parts, represent the condensed, archaically distorted fusion of both parental images in the son's delusional system. God, in this system, would then be the delusional composite of both father and mother. No doubt, the father's usurpation of the maternal role compounded this fused image in the son's mind and formed a breeding ground for later distortions.

The discovery of new material regarding the patient's family would tend to support this impression. His mother, *Pauline* (née Haase), was herself the third child of a prominent physician and professor of medicine in Leipzig, precisely as was her son *Paul*, our patient, who during his illness delusionally changed his sex to that of the mother and hallucinated about being "Miss Schreber." In other words, he changed himself delusionally from *Paul* to *Pauline*.

Another example of Schreber's confusion regarding both his own sexual identity and the identity of paternal and maternal figures is shown in the following data from the municipal archives in Leipzig: the maternal grand-

4 See pp. 151–154.

mother of the patient was *Juliana Emilia Haase,* wife of the prominent physician-professor mentioned above. In the *Memoirs* the patient transforms his grandmother into a practicing male physician named *Julius Emil Haase.* On the basis of documentary material extending over a century of the Schreber genealogy, no such male person of this name existed in his lineage. We are confronted here with a delusional change of sex similar, though in reverse, to the patient's own change of sex during his psychosis. He employs the same reversal, narcissistically elaborated, in the case of his paternal grandmother whose name was *Friederike (née Grosse)*; in a delusional footnote she becomes *Friedrich der Grosse.* This footnote (in Chapter II of the *Memoirs*) also deals with the delusionally exalted lineage of the Flechsig and Schreber families and mentions an occurrence "between perhaps earlier generations of the Schreber and Flechsig families which amounted to soul murder."

According to information from the *Stadtarchiv* Leipzig, the grandmother Friederike died on December 30, 1846, and it is likely that this was for our 4½-year-old patient a first experience with the death of a close family member.

When we consider Schreber's division of God into an upper and lower one or into a superior and inferior deity, named Ormuzd and Ahriman, respectively, and spoken of by the patient as the "hierarchy of God's realms," the role of his elder (and only) brother in the structure of this delusional aggregate should be recalled. Freud mentioned the probability that Schreber's peculiarly composed God had derived from paternal and fraternal roots contained in the delusional material. The new data confirm Freud's assumption. The brother, Gustav, who after the father's sudden death in 1861 became the head of the Schreber family, committed suicide in 1877, a few weeks after his promotion to *Gerichtsrat* (judge) at a provincial Saxon court in Bautzen. With regard to the mode of suicide, I quote verbatim from the *Stadtarchiv-Bautzen* in Saxony, which has the following entry in its collection of municipal documents for the year 1877: "Schreber, Daniel Gustav, Doctor of Law, Royal Judge in Bautzen, according to church register St. Peter, Bautzen, died on 8 May, in the morning, 38 years old, unmarried. *Suicide by gunshot.*" (Italics added.)

Several newspapers in Saxony carried similar notices under the date of May 10, 1877, and one mentioned that melancholia or depression must be regarded "as the cause of the sad event" (*Chemnitzer Tageblatt*, May 10, 1877). This newspaper emphasizes further that the suicide occurred only a short time after the brother's nomination. I consider this last point as well as the obituaries in the newspapers important, since Schreber delusionally indicates in the *Memoirs* that he read *his own death notice* in the newspaper and that his 1893 breakdown occurred a short time after his promotion to the post of *Senatspräsident.* The identification aspects and their far-reaching effects are particularly impressive; various cross-identifications are readily discernible in Schreber's pathology. In the *Memoirs* they are often expressed by the occurrence of certain names, dates, and more specifically by anniversary reactions.

The sister's letter is of further interest with respect to other aspects of Schreber's symptomatology. She describes in some detail how everything in the Schreber home was *Gottwärts gerichtet* (oriented toward God), how God was present in their childhood world at all times, not merely in their daily prayers, but in all their feeling, thinking, and doings. She concludes with the words: "All this was finished with the sudden death of our beloved father . . . our childhood Paradise was destroyed." This statement may be viewed as a nondelusional version of her brother's archaic "end-of-the-world" fantasy. It is in sharp contrast to his delusional attempt to recapture the lost childhood paradise through a reunion with God-father-mother-brother, that is, through the formation of his particular God-aggregate of upper and lower parts, anterior and posterior courts.

The great number of Schreber's "divine miracles" derived from early paternal manipulations, can be understood as complex manifestations of a compelling, regressively reinstinctualized need to recover or recreate the lost objects, something we frequently encounter in certain transference reactions of a stormy nature. Schreber's transference reactions to his physician Dr. Flechsig and the doctor's assistants and orderlies, are graphically described in the *Memoirs* and served Freud as valuable landmarks in his analysis of the case. The father of the patient was indeed an extraordinary man. Some of the passages about religion in the elder Schreber's books read as though written by one who, while not an ordained priest and not fond of dogma, had seen the true light of God.

In studying his writings, I found he was fond of lecturing and sermonizing to his children on the human body, the wonders of nature, and the relation of God to the universe, elaborating especially on the phenomena of magnetic attraction and repulsion in which he saw the expression of basic cosmic forces governing the universe. On these phenomena of attraction and repulsion he built a sort of popularized pseudophilosophical system of his own, his *Weltanschauung* (concept of the world), and wrote and lectured about it extensively. The paternal *Weltanschauung* reappears in the son's delusional cosmology. Though distorted, condensed, and concretized, it emerges throughout the text of the *Memoirs* in readily recognizable fashion as a conglomeration of philosophical, theological, and cosmological speculations in which divine rays, attraction to and repulsion by God, magic attributes of the deity, personal "nerve contact" with the latter, and similar ideas predominate. The nondelusional raw material of most of this can be found in the father's medical and philosophical writings. For example, in discussing the span of human life on earth, the father indicates 200 years as the maximum age that human beings may attain in time to come. The son's delusional description of the end of the world contains this figure as the approximate time limit set by him for the occurrence of the anticipated event. Again, one of the father's books is entitled *Anthropos: Der Wunderbau des menschlichen Organismus* (The Miraculous Structure of the Human Organism). The term *Wunder* appears in the *Memoirs* in constant connection with God's miracles, that is, the father's "miraculous medical" performances; it is also quoted almost directly by the son as *wundervoller Aufbau* (wonderful structure) and then explained by him in an almost insight-revealing footnote: "Again an expression which I did not invent . . . the term *wundervoller Aufbau* was suggested to me from outside."

From the sister's letter and other sources the origin of these notions becomes clear. The father, a passionate educator and eloquent talker, took his children on frequent strolls, citing to them, with paternal pride and sermonizing insistence, the *wonders* of God, of the world, and of the body. During and after such lectures the children were questioned in minute detail as to their understanding of the cited *wonders* and paternal praise was bestowed upon the child who, like our overobedient patient, knew the correct answers.

In discussing the onset of Schreber's first illness, Freud pointed only to Schreber's passing remark about his candidature for the *Reichstag* in 1884. In this connection, I wish to supply some of the following data. Schreber was then running for the *Reichstag* as the avowed candidate of the *National-liberale Partei* (National Liberal party), which was in opposition to Bismarck's autocratic and reactionary régime in Germany. After a political campaign in which Schreber actively participated, the election took place on October 28, 1884. He was defeated, with an overwhelming majority voting against him (14,512 against 5,762). A local newspaper in his election district —Chemnitz in Saxony—carried the scornful headline about his candidature: *"Wer kennt schon den Dr. Schreber?"* (Who, After All, Knows Dr. Schreber?)

A few weeks later, in November, 1884, he fell ill for the first time, and in December of the same year was hospitalized for about six months. He considered himself incurable, had difficulties in talking and walking, and made two suicide attempts. It is clear from the hospital records that depressive and hypochondriacal manifestations were present and that the depression was connected at least chronologically with his election defeat, which must have constituted a formidable narcissistic injury for him. The speech and walking disturbances might well have been related to his active participation in the election campaign.

Schreber's reaction to his political defeat could have been intensified by events going back to his early life. There is evidence that the Schreber family was in political difficulties during the 1840s, especially during the revolutionary years 1847 and 1848, when the patient was 5 years old. The turbulent political events in Germany during the 1880s seem to have revived in him memories and anxieties connected with his childhood experiences during the late 1840s and to have contributed, in connection with his political campaign of 1884, to a regressively intensified reliving of the castration fears of his oedipal years, which likewise had been marked by political events and the related uncertainty.

Turning to the outbreak of Schreber's second and lasting illness, its chronological connection with his promotion to *Senatspräsident* has been duly noted and often commented on in the literature. But here a second, perhaps equally important, factor must be added. Schreber's brother, Gustav, as we have seen, committed suicide a short time after his nomination as *Gerichtsrat*; the patient, Daniel Paul, tried to do the same a few weeks after his nomination to an even higher juridical position and, prevented from physical suicide, succumbed to lifelong mental illness.

12 / Schreber and Flechsig: A Further Contribution to the "Kernel of Truth" in Schreber's Delusional System[1]

The *Memoirs* contain lengthy and recurrent references to "God's personal distance and remoteness." Schreber tells us the deity adopted this attitude in relation to him, the patient, and to men in general. After the creation of the world, God "retired to an enormous distance" and considered it dangerous to draw close to mankind, though there was "no danger . . . in approaching corpses." The danger for God, then, consisted in His contact with *living* human beings, contact which occurred only after their death.

In the archaic transference relationship with Dr. Flechsig, his physician,[2] Schreber likewise describes such phenomena, including Dr. Flechsig's self-removal. He writes that Dr. Flechsig had performed experiments on him *at a distance,* at one point breaking off the experiment entirely. Furthermore, Flechsig's soul had ascended to heaven prematurely, without the patient's knowledge or consent.

Much of this appears explainable in terms of the patient's psychotic withdrawal and isolation. Historically speaking, it can be understood in terms of the sudden deaths of both father and brother. But there is more to it. In one passage of the *Memoirs* the patient mentions that God is likely to "annihilate" a human being who embarrasses him and that God will strike out, *if a human being gets too close to him,* no matter how good or innocuous the intent of a person may be. In analyzing these and similar passages and relating them to other source material, I see in them archaically distorted allusions to earlier crucial events involving actual and disruptive changes in Schreber's family setting.

It will be recalled that when the patient was 15 or 16 years of age, his father sustained a serious skull injury. There is evidence that during the years following the injury until close to his death, *the father lived in partial seclusion* and withdrew not only from his many activities but from personal contact with his children as well. There is reason to believe that the previously so vigorous and active man could not tolerate the idea of being seen

[1] This is a condensed version of the original paper, which appeared in the *Journal of the American Psychoanalytic Association*, Vol. 16, No. 4 (July, 1968).

[2] Dr. Paul Theodor Flechsig, professor of psychiatry at the University of Leipzig, and one of the leading European specialists from 1872 to 1927.

in his reduced physical condition. He apparently also had *Tobsuchtsanfälle*, that is, violent outbursts of rage and fury, and the report about him says, *"Seine Frau . . . war oft der einzige Mensch, den er um sich duldete"* (His wife was often the only human being whom he tolerated around himself). One of Schreber's sisters was the source of this information.

It is my impression, then, that some of God's peculiar characteristics and unintelligible attitudes, which He so conspicuously exhibited, can now be better understood: God's personal remoteness and retirement to an almost inaccessible distance, his withdrawal from contact with human beings, his strange difficulties and idiosyncrasies toward people and certain situations, his vulnerability to close contact with men, and his tendency to strike out "if a human being gets too close to him." These strange attributes of Schreber's God can be seen, I believe, as derivatives of the patient's experiences in the Schreber home. Quite suddenly—after the earlier oversolicitous, symbiotically tinged and subjectively overpowering father-son relationship throughout childhood—the father withdrew from contact with Schreber during his mid-adolescence. This development abruptly and unexpectedly followed *the skull or brain injury*, which left the formerly all-powerful father partially disabled both physically and emotionally. It likewise ended with the father's sudden death.

Freud has already stressed that the God of Schreber's *Memoirs* is a sort of weak and oddly insecure deity. He also pointed to the son's positively toned attitude toward this deity, despite the strong ambivalence that frequently emerges in Schreber's text. Much of this is reflected in the later patient-doctor relationship, that is, in the transference situation with Dr. Flechsig. Although the transference phenomena during Schreber's illness contain features of the deepest regression, several bear the stamp of the traumatic events mentioned above. The *Memoirs* initially depict Flechsig as having had "a remarkable eloquence which affected me deeply" (Schreber's father was an eloquent speaker). He is subsequently described as holding himself aloof (as God did), as threatening to abandon Schreber, and as performing hypnotic experiments on him *from a distance*. Later Flechsig vanished entirely, became a "Flechsig-soul" and a "Flechsig-god," an unexpected change that resulted in his not "seeing Professor Flechsig again." In another passage Schreber records: "I also saw—in a dream vision—his [Flechsig's] funeral procession from his house toward the Thonberg," an almost unmistakable allusion to the father's and probably also the elder brother's funerals, both of whom had died without warning. Kitay has noted the connection with the brother's death and funeral (63). Actually, Dr. Flechsig died only in 1927, many years after Schreber's demise in 1911.

On the basis of our knowledge of the father's withdrawal and grossly disturbed behavior during his last years of life, culminating in his transportation to and sudden death in a university hospital in Leipzig, I believe we can recognize in Schreber's archaic transference fantasies the regressively distorted, though identifiable vestiges of his concrete life experiences. That is, we have now uncovered with the aid of a posthumous mining operation the "kernel of truth" contained in such delusional formations.

The "bellowing miracle," mentioned in various chapters of the *Memoirs*, may ultimately likewise be connected with those experiences that represent in part the father's introjected-projected outbursts of rage and noisy behavior as well as the son's helpless longing and protest when "God retired to an enormous distance." The patient has this to say about the bellowing:

> . . . however little I intend to lend any personal acrimony to the following description, an account of how unbearably I suffered during this stay in the cells, nonetheless belongs to the complete picture of the story of my sufferings. My sleep is . . . exclusively *dependent on the heavenly constellations;* sleep becomes impossible for me as soon as *God has withdrawn to too great a distance, which happens periodically for half a day or at least several hours* . . . for over twelve months, more or less *severe states of bellowing* . . . occur *whenever I cannot convince the distant God,* who believes I have become demented, that this is not so. (Italics added.)

Such expressions of protest, especially those concerning God's periodic withdrawals for periods of time during the day, accord well with the information about the father's ill health after the accident, partial seclusion ("withdrawal"), and recurrent periods of rest. The italicized passages illustrate the connection between the episodes of withdrawal and the states of bellowing. At the same time, the patient's real and rage-provoking experience in the Sonnenstein sanatorium should not be overlooked.

In view of what appears to have been a serious brain sydrome from which the father suffered toward the end of his life, it also becomes understandable that Schreber thought—on entering Flechsig's clinic—that he had a brain disease himself—more precisely, "softening of the brain"—and that he would soon die. This belief may have been reinforced by certain circumstances belonging to the transference.

Dr. Flechsig's office was decorated with impressive pictorializations of the human brain. His career as a psychiatrist had started with important anatomical studies on the brainstem and spinal cord. One of his early achievements had been a postmortem procedure on the human brain, which he called *Coup de Flechsig* (Flechsig's cut), an autopsy technique he developed as early as 1872. Dr. Flechsig seems to have been proud of this; for later as a famous neuropathologist and neuroanatomist he spoke of it in lectures and publications, the latter filled with anatomical illustrations, pictures of sagittal, frontal, and horizontal sections of the brain, nerve fibers, and other neuroanatomic structures. Included among his later achievements was the discovery of a section of the spinal tract named for him—*"Flechsig's bundle"*—which made him world famous.

For the analyst it comes as no surprise, therefore, that the first chapter of the *Memoirs* opens with a reference to "the nerves of the body" and then continues with the statement "God to start with is only nerve. . . ." In the light of Flechsig's prominence as a *pathologist* actively engaged in dissecting and examining corpses, Schreber's repeated remarks that *God deals mainly with corpses* acquire added significance.

Another outstanding feature in Schreber's multifaceted symptomatology has been his intense castration fear. The overwhelming concreteness of this fear and the subjective conviction of penile shrinkage or disappearance that Schreber developed when he entered Flechsig's hospital, prompted me to search for further data.

In studying Dr. Flechsig's life and work, I came upon an autobiographical sketch (it is not only patients who write autobiographical accounts) and a series of medical papers by Flechsig. Besides testifying to their author's high academic position and notable scientific output, they are of more than casual interest to the psychiatrist and analyst working on the Schreber case. In them Dr. Flechsig, then medical director of the very institution in which Schreber was hospitalized, describes *the use of actual castration in his hospital as a method to be employed for the cure of serious nervous and psychological ailments.*

One paper, published in the *Neurologisches Zentralblatt* (Leipzig) in 1884, reports three cases of castration performed in the psychiatric institution he headed and discusses in scholarly detail the "favorable results . . . in depressive, manic, and mildly paranoid conditions" obtained with this type of treatment. Dr. Flechsig then proposes further "to develop the indications for the use of castration as a treatment of neuroses and psychoses" at his clinic, since the current views in regard to the "value of castration as a means against neuroses and psychoses still vary considerably." At his own clinic, he concludes, the castrations were performed by one of the assistants under his supervision, and the clinical results were uniformly good. To be sure, the patients described in Dr. Flechsig's report were *female;* but at no point are the indications limited as to sex or mental condition. The paper speaks of castration as a useful method in mental or emotional disorders generally, with special reference to depressive, manic, and paranoid states. It suggests the continued, possibly even expanded application of castrative surgery at the Flechsig clinic in the years following its publication in 1884.

Thus, the "kernel of truth" that emerges with respect to the patient's enormous castration fear on entering that hospital, also turns out to be one of considerable proportion. No one can say with certainty whether the castrative practices used at Flechsig's clinic were known to Schreber or whether the patient was familiar with Dr. Flechsig's writings. I am inclined to believe he was. Schreber read voraciously and was particularly interested in scientific and medical literature. In the *Memoirs* he quotes extensively from psychiatric textbooks and frequently refers to nerve fibers, nerve tissue, neurological structures, spinal *tracts* and *bundles*.

Leipzig was a comparatively small city at that time, and Dr. Flechsig's reputation was worldwide. Members of the Russian Czarist family and other royalty came to him as patients. In the year following Schreber's second hospitalization at Flechsig's—this was the popular name for the clinic throughout Leipzig—Dr. Flechsig became *Rector Magnificus* of the ancient Leipzig University. In this way, he ascended almost literally to the "God"-like position that the author of the *Memoirs* ascribes to him. Since Dr. Flechsig's own books and papers were published in Leipzig, it seems more likely than not that Schreber had at least a general knowledge of them and that some notion about castration as a specific method for *Nervenkranke* in use at Flechsig's clinic had reached the patient at one time or another. Indeed, it is my impression that Schreber, not unlike other psychiatric patients, must have read his doctor's medical writings in great detail.

In addition to what was said above, textual and contextual evidence can be adduced to demonstrate the accuracy of this assumption. Many of Dr. Flechsig's scientific papers contain references to and descriptions of certain neuroanatomical tracts in the brain that he calls *Strahlen* (rays). The photograph of Dr. Flechsig in his office shows on the wall behind him a giant brain. In studying Schreber's autobiographical account, one encounters the term "rays" numerous times, usually in direct or at least close contextual relation

Figure 12 / Dr. Paul Theodor Flechsig in his office.

to God (father). In one of his fantasies Schreber makes the rays enter his own body. To the same cluster of ideas belongs Schreber's affinity to the rays of the sun, a symbol whose maleness in the total context of the *Memoirs* has been confirmed through Laffal's linguistic research.

The bitter complaint that God does not really understand living men, that he deals only with corpses, must ultimately, in accordance with Freud's interpretation, be a reproach addressed by the sick son to the father. However, in the transference setting, it must also refer to Dr. Flechsig. Schreber's intense preoccupation with God, Protestantism, religious problems, immortality, soul, brain, and even piano playing, are likewise transference phenomena. To wit: Dr. Flechsig himself was an accomplished pianist and president of the Franz Liszt Association in Leipzig. His family were in close friendship with the famous composer and musician Robert Schumann. His father was a dedicated Protestant minister and theologian in Saxony. And finally, to complete the transference picture, the title of the twice-published lecture given by Dr. Flechsig when he became *Rector Magnificus* was "Brain and Soul."[3]

[3] A brief explanatory note concerning the term "soul" is indicated: in contemporary thinking it connotes essentially a religious-theological concept. But in Flechsig's and Schreber's time the word "soul" was widely used in academic writings. It was employed, especially in the German psychological literature, to designate a variety of mental processes, such as perceptive and sensorial functions, reflex actions, voluntary and involuntary neurophysiological mechanisms, and other phenomena belonging to the nervous system.

13 / The Schreber Case: Sixty Years Later

In summing up the multifaceted material presented in this volume, the place and significance of the Schreber case for present-day psychoanalysis, psychiatry, psychology, and psychohistory can now be condensed in the following way:

1. Schreber's autobiography constitutes an erudite layman's account of his psychotic illness, a sort of treasure chest filled with rich and fascinating information for every analytic student.
2. Freud's analysis is a textbook of psychodynamic discoveries and analytic formulations in the field of psychotic illness, with emphasis on the unconscious dynamics operative in the paranoid personality. His chief concern was the elucidation of drive and defense in this type of mental abnormality.
3. Since Freud's inquiry consisted in the application of psychoanalysis to the productions of a patient who described his experiences in a candid, self-revealing manner, it is in essence a clinical study. Freud arrived at his conclusions through methodical analytic insight and research. His understanding was in no way derived from this particular document alone. Rather, it had been acquired previously in the course of his clinical investigation of patients who suffered from the disease.
4. With regard to the analytic exploration of an autobiographical account, Freud explained that paranoia "is precisely a disorder in which a written report or printed case history can take the place of personal acquaintance with the patient." In view of the known secretiveness and marked retience[1] displayed by such patients in personal contact with the interviewer, Freud's perceptive statement appears as justified today as it was in 1911.
5. Further scientific contributions have sharpened our understanding of many aspects of the case and clarified the meaning of numerous previously incomprehensible details of the case history. These studies illustrate that the contents of the *Memoirs* have been examined from a variety of viewpoints.

The Schreber analysis, as an entity, was a seminal event. The unraveling of the patient's bizarre and cryptic narrative—which without Freud's decoding would presumably have remained an obscure text gathering dust in some remote archival niche—has not only given impetus to much follow-up research,

---

[1] For a clinical example, see p. 111.

but has also initiated significant advances with respect to our knowledge of psychotic illness. The finding that paranoid patients project onto others the blame for what they regard as blameworthy in themselves, was especially fruitful. It opened pathways through which ambulatory and hospitalized patients alike could be approached therapeutically, that is, by helping them to gain insight into the causes and meaning of their subjective experiences.

The concept of restitution has recently been scrutinized anew and it has been proposed by Arlow and Brenner (3) that delusional and hallucinatory phenomena be related to disturbed ego functioning, that is, the ego's outspoken disorganization in psychotic illness. In such states fantasies, experienced as real, become delusions and, if sensory elements prevail, hallucinations. According to Federn misperceptions of reality can occur long before the actual break with it; the illness itself is seen not as resulting from a defensive struggle but rather as "a defeat of an ego which has ceased to be able to defend itself. . . ." Freeman, on the other hand, in accordance with Freud's interpretation, views the weakening of the individual's ties (decathexis) to the object world as the essential feature in schizophrenia. Other approaches are possible, but Freud's thinking regarding regression, defense, and restitution, in my opinion, provides the most comprehensive framework for the understanding of the multiple phenomena involved.

To return to the defensive, restorative trends recognized by Freud in Schreber's psychosis, it is evident that they did not lead to *restitutio ad integrum*. Hazardous though it may be to reconstruct what went on in the patient's mind, it can be noted that the restitutional strivings[2], supported by an encompassing intellect, expressed themselves both in his creative work and in "miracling-up" significant experiences of his early life. In his search to reestablish the links to the object world, the patient recathected and retraced the lost father-son relationship by means of his delusional formations. In them he recaptured the image of the ambivalently loved/hated father, meeting him face to face, voice to voice (in the bellowing miracle), and body part to body part (in the head and chest compression miracles, and so on).

In this context, Pollock's investigation[3] of anniversary reactions as "indicators of past unresolved traumas" and Volkan's observations on the "linking objects of pathological mourners" are relevant. These psychological processes provide means whereby lost object relationships with the deceased can be magically maintained or reestablished. The psychic reverberations resulting from the losses sustained can be identified by studying such specific emotional responses to trauma and unresolved grief. Schreber's persistent references to the *wonders* that God performed on him and that we have recognized as repressed realistic traumata can be seen in the same light. The father's

---

[2] The writing of the *Memoirs* undoubtedly was a recuperative act.

[3] G. H. Pollack, "Temporal Anniversary Manifestations: Hour, Day, Holiday," *The Psychoanalytic Quarterly*, Vol. 40, No. 1 (1971), 123–131.

last book, published while he was still alive, has *Wunderbau* (*wonder*ful structure or edifice) in its title. The incessant return of the term *Wunder* in the son's writing thus presents, in addition to its other meanings, a memento to the father's final literary work.

Withal, it should be borne in mind that schizophrenia in its various forms and diagnostic labels (paranoid, catatonic, simplex) remains a vast and perplexing problem beset by a plethora of unresolved issues. There is, at present, no universally accepted theory concerning the causation of the illness (or illnesses). Many researchers—not excluding Freud—have expressed the opinion that the psychotic enters this world with a basic ego weakness, that is, a malapparatus (5) that may predispose him to the disease. While Freud stressed the practical and therapeutic value of the psychological approach, he nonetheless throughout his life maintained his belief in the biological substrata of mental functions. He wrote (44): "The phenomena with which we have had to deal do not belong only to psychology. . . . They have also an organic and biological aspect."

As shown in the chapter on Schreber's father, the latter was a sick man. In the probably autobiographical fragment cited on page 64, he spoke of his morbid state as a young man. Certainly in his activities as a reformer of apostolic fervor as well as in the upbringing of his offspring, he exhibited pathological propensities, not to mention the cerebral symptoms that appeared toward the end of his life. On the basis of clinical observations, Eissler (18) reports that "frequently schizophrenics . . . grow up with a parent who was bizarre and pathologically compulsive."

In vulnerable individuals, notably at such times of stress as puberty, postpuberty, climacterium, and emotional strain resulting from traumatic and other precipitating events, regressive tendencies may develop either rapidly or slowly and insidiously to a state of serious, archaically tinged mental disorganization. Among the common clinical consequences are weakening of reality testing, loss of ego boundaries, and regressive alterations in ego functioning.

The recent proliferation of popular writings on schizophrenia has fostered the promulgation of a conspirational theory of psychosis. These writings would have us believe that the patient's parents (and, in a broader sense, family, society, environment) are the true culprits and should be condemned as "persecutors." No doubt these texts provide interesting reading matter for popular consumption. But they take into consideration neither the parents' own emotional problems nor the deeper processes underlying mental development and functioning. The conspirational theory, reminiscent of Schreber's ideas of persecutory activities on the deity's part, is simplistic and reductionist. To attribute conspirational activities or "plots" to certain groups—Jews, Jesuits, blacks, Tories, Freemasons—is an age-old scapegoating phenomenon with which we are all unhappily familiar. Today it is the parents' turn.

The pathological implications of growing up in an environment deprived of close, personal, and emotionally responsive interaction have been demonstrated in numerous studies. However, our data with regard to Schreber's upbringing indicate a different setting. He came from a milieu dominated by an autocratic and charismatic parent whose harsh, controlling, and cruel behavior must have produced in the growing child feelings of fear, awe, inadequacy, and guilt. The anxiety-producing factors included severely imposed discipline, use of devices for terrifying children into submission, and emphasis on inflexibly enforced performance, rather than a lack of closeness or communication. That excessive parental influence can smother a child is hardly a new finding. From all we now know about Schreber's first 40 years or so, he had developed and remained well until the outbreak of his first disease. Nonetheless, throughout childhood he had been subjected to an overload of physical and emotional "input," an intensely exaggerated interaction between father and son—something resembling a mutually shared drama of a despotic "godlike" parent figure on the one side and a pathetically helpless child on the other.

The present stage of psychoanalytic knowledge cannot fully explain how Schreber could have led a successful life in apparently good mental health for four decades. It may be that the young Schreber, faced with a father of brute superiority, obtained a measure of inner support from his feelings of identification and belongingness. The father's concept of children as personal property is clearly expressed in his writings; he acted out his ideas and techniques on the son's body. Erikson has discussed some of them in his study of Martin Luther's relationship with his harsh father who likewise applied "mental and corporeal terror" in the upbringing of the religious reformer.

As already indicated, at the time of the Schreber analysis, the study of aggression had received scant attention in psychoanalysis. Still today, the analytic theory of aggression is less well developed than the theory of sexuality. Psychoanalysis has not yet fully charted the paths taken by the sexual and aggressive drives in seeking contact through fused-affectionate, predominantly hostile, or sharply separate expressions. The same holds true of nonanalytic investigations of aggressive behavior that, in a broad sense, is usually equated with attack and/or violence. As for the gross manifestations of aggression this is certainly so. On closer scrutiny, though, behavior designated as aggression poses a good many questions: Is aggression part of the organism's innate endowment? Is it resorted to when other outlets for activity are blocked? Is it a defense against passivity? Is it always a response to frustration and oppression?

Some observers hold that aggression is essentially constructive—that is, in the service of mastery—but that it may become destructive when it is eroticized. The latter point leads us back to the Schreber case and the repressed sexual conflict elucidated by Freud. The attentive reader will recall that Schreber, bellowing at the sun, called it a "whore." Interestingly, the literal meaning of the word "aggression" points to this connection; derived from the Latin *ad gradire* (to move toward someone, to get near an object), it denotes verbally the very mutuality that we unveiled in the Schreber father-son situation.

The *Memoirs* contains many episodes of explosive aggression, outbursts of rage, roaring exclamations ("bellowing"), and fights. Some of these episodes involve hospital personnel and other patients. A more subtle type of aggression may have been implied in Schreber's archaic parturition fantasies, which were emphasized by Macalpine and Hunter. Such fantasies, often expressed in psychophysiological symptoms, have a close relation to the individual's narcissism. They can lead to malignant pathological states. The paranoid's equation of persecutor and feces belongs to the same area of conflict.

The weight of evidence points to psychological causes in the emergence of paranoid states, with repressed homosexuality and hostility as etiological elements. How deep the emotional tie to his father had been is shown by the anniversary reaction mentioned earlier: when Schreber is called upon to assume a prominent "father" role as *Senatspräsident*, the conflicts of libidinal and aggressive origin that had been repressed for 32 years break through, and he falls ill on the very date his father had died. Sometime thereafter Schreber began to speak directly to God—the deified father.

Not every patient displays Schreber's paranoid turmoil during the first stages of his illness. An early clinical diagnosis, relatively simple in the majority of cases, can sometimes present a problem. I refer, by way of example, to a clinical observation that goes back a number of years. The patient who consulted me was a young and charming woman, well educated and interested in the arts, music, singing, and dancing. The wife of a professional, she described for nearly an hour her husband's lack of consideration, uncooperativeness, personal coldness, sexual aloofness, and sundry other deficiencies. Much of what she said sounded reasonable, if somewhat angry and exaggerated—the way a disappointed wife who feels rejected might justifiably complain about her husband's behavior. When the interview ended, I had not yet arrived at a definite diagnosis. As I rose and accompanied the patient to the door, she continued to pour out her complaints. Finally, at the door, she confided her long-withheld secret. Lowering her voice to a whisper, she said, ". . . and I must tell you, doctor, that my husband has our home surrounded by 12 detectives who watch every step of mine from morning to evening. . . ." This, of course, solved the diagnostic problem, though—admittedly—I never found out why the number of detectives employed by the husband was 12.

The anxiety and suspiciousness expressed by this female patient can be supplemented by an example from the treatment history of a sorely troubled male patient with murderous fantasies, whose extreme hostility emerged in the transference setting with full force. The picture shown here (Figure 13), painted by this patient, illustrates his violent feelings with impressive clarity.

Figure 13 / In this painting by a male patient with paranoid fantasies, towering rage is expressed by the image of a prehistoric, dangerous monster (the omnipotent, voracious "Id") emerging out of the otherwise empty skull. Note the enormous oral and anal features of the monster; also note the narcissistic grandiosity; the prehistoric beast represents TYRANNOSAURUS REX, the most powerful of all dinosaurs.

Though he graphically depicted his own emotional state of extreme hostility and suspicion, the face does not bear any resemblance to his actual appearance. Analytic treatment helped him gain awareness of and insight into the unconscious dynamics of his disorder, and proved curative.

In my opinion, it was through Freud's pioneering Schreber analysis that these unconscious dynamics were explored and thus made accessible to analytic-therapeutic intervention. Schreber, then, became a seminal figure himself, who paradoxically through his *Memoirs* and the fantasies he communicated contributed to our understanding of his illness and in a broader sense of the nature of man.

Bibliography for Parts I and II

1. Abraham, K. (1908), "The Psycho-Sexual Differences between Hysteria and Dementia Praecox." In *Selected Papers of Karl Abraham*. New York: Basic Books, 1953, pp. 64–79.
2. Allen, T. E. (1967), "Suicidal Impulse in Depression and Paranoia." *Int. J. Psycho-Anal.*, 48:3, 433–438.
3. Arlow, J., and Brenner, C. (1969), "The Psychopathology of the Psychoses: A Proposed Revision." *Int. J. Psycho-Anal.*, 50:1, 5–14.
4. Bak, R. C. (1946), "Masochism in Paranoia." *Psychoanal. Quart.*, 15:285–301.
5. ——— (1972), "Object Relationships in Schizophrenia and Perversions." *Newsletter, Brooklyn Psychiat. Soc.*, 6:3, 2–3.
6. Baumeyer, F. (1956), "The Schreber Case." *Int. J. Psycho-Anal.*, 37:61–74.
7. ——— (1973), "Nachträge zum Fall Schreber." In *Bürgerliche Wahnwelt um Neunzehnhundert*. Wiesbaden: Focus-Verlag.
8. Bellak, L. (1960), "The Treatment of Schizophrenia and Psychoanalytic Theory." *J. of Nerv. and Ment. Dis.*, 131:39–46.
9. ——— and Loeb, L. (1969), *The Schizophrenic Syndrome*. New York: Grune & Stratton.
10. Bleuler, E. (1911), *Dementia Praecox or the Group of Schizophrenias*. New York: Int. Univ. Press., 1950.
11. Bonner, H. (1951), "The Problem of Diagnosis in Paranoic Disorder." *Amer. J. Psych.*, 107:677–683.
12. Boyer, L. B. (1967), "Office Treatment of Schizophrenic Patients." In *Psychoanalytic Treatment of Schizophrenic and Characterological Disorders*. New York: Science House.
13. Brenner, C. (1971), "The Psychoanalytic Concept of Aggression." *Int. J. Psycho-Anal.*, 52:137–144.
14. Cameron, N. (1959), "Paranoid Conditions and Paranoia." In *American Handbook of Psychiatry*, edited by S. Arieti. New York: Basic Books.
15. ——— (1967), "Paranoid Reactions." In *Comprehensive Textbook of Psychiatry*, edited by A. M. Freedman and H. I. Kaplan. Baltimore: Williams & Wilkins.
16. Casati, G. (1891), *Zehn Jahre in Equatoria und die Rückkehr von Emin Pasha*. Bamberg: Reinhardt & Stottner.
17. Ehrenwald, J. (1960), "The Symbiotic Matrix of Paranoid Delusions and the Homosexual Alternative." *Amer. J. Psychoan.*, 20:49–65.

18. Eissler, K. R. (1953), "Notes upon the Emotionality of a Schizophrenic Patient." *Psychoanal. Study Child*, 8:199–251.
19. ——— (1963), *Goethe: A Psychoanalytic Study*. Detroit: Wayne State Univ. Press.
20. Erikson, E. H. (1958), *Young Man Luther*. New York: W. W. Norton.
21. Fairbairn, R. W. (1956), "Considerations Arising Out of the Schreber Case." *Brit. J. Med. Psychol.*, 29:113–127.
22. Federn, P. (1952), *Ego Psychology and the Psychoses*. New York: Basic Books.
23. Fenichel, O. (1945), *The Psychoanalytic Theory of Neurosis*. New York: W. W. Norton.
24. Flechsig, P. T. (1878), *Über System Erkrankungen im Rückenmark*. Leipzig: Wigand.
25. ——— (1884), "Zur Gynäkologischen Behandlung der Hysterie." *Neurol. Zentralblatt*, 19/20:1–18.
26. ——— (1896), "Gehirn und Seele." *Rektoratsrede*. Leipzig: Veit.
27. Freeman, T. (1970), "The Psychopathology of the Psychoses: A Reply to Arlow and Brenner." *Int. J. Psycho-Anal.*, 51:407–415.
28. Freud, S. (1889), "Screen Memories." *Standard Ed.*, 3:303–322. London: Hogarth Press, 1962.
29. ——— (1894), "The Neuro-Psychoses of Defense." *Standard Ed.*, 3:45–61. London: Hogarth Press, 1962.
30. ——— (1896), "Further Remarks on the Neuro-Psychoses of Defense." *Standard Ed.*, 3:162–185. London: Hogarth Press, 1962.
31. ——— (1900), *The Interpretation of Dreams. Standard Ed.*, 4 and 5. London: Hogarth Press, 1953.
32. ——— (1905), "Three Essays on the Theory of Sexuality." *Standard Ed.*, 7:130–243. London: Hogarth Press, 1953.
33. ——— (1907), "Delusions and Dreams in Jensen's *Gradiva*." *Standard Ed.*, 9:7–95. London: Hogarth Press, 1959.
34. ——— (1911a), "Psycho-Analytic Notes upon an Autobiographical Account of a Case of Paranoia (Dementia Paranoides)." *Standard Ed.*, 12:9–82. London: Hogarth Press, 1958.
35. ——— (1911b), "Formulations on the Two Principles of Mental Functioning." *Standard Ed.*, 12:218–226. London: Hogarth Press, 1958.
36. ——— (1914), "On Narcissism: An Introduction." *Standard Ed.*, 14:73–102. London: Hogarth Press, 1957.
37. ——— (1915a), "Observations on Transference-Love." *Standard Ed.*, 12:159–171. London: Hogarth Press, 1958.
38. ——— (1915b), "The Unconscious." *Standard Ed.*, 14:166–204. London: Hogarth Press, 1957.
39. ——— (1922), "Some Neurotic Mechanisms in Jealousy, Paranoia, and Homosexuality." *Collected Papers*, 2:232–243. London: Hogarth Press, 1948.
40. ——— (1923), *The Ego and the Id. Standard Ed.*, 19. London: Hogarth Press, 1961.
41. ——— (1924), "The Loss of Reality in Neurosis and Psychosis." *Standard Ed.*, 19:183–187. London: Hogarth Press, 1961.
42. ——— (1933), *New Introductory Lectures on Psycho-Analysis. Standard Ed.*, 22. London: Hogarth Press, 1964.

43. ——— (1938), "Constructions in Analysis." *Collected Papers*, 5:358–371. London: Hogarth Press, 1953.

44. ——— (1940), *An Outline of Psycho-Analysis. Standard Ed.*, 23. London: Hogarth Press, 1964.

45. ——— (1966), *The Letters of Sigmund Freud and Karl Abraham.* Selected and edited by Ernst L. Freud. New York: Basic Books.

46. Fromm-Reichmann, F. (1954), "Psychotherapy of Schizophrenia." *Amer. J. Psych.*, 111:410–419.

47. Garma, A. (1971), "Within the Realm of the Death Instinct." *Int. J. Psycho-Anal.*, 52:145–154.

48. Gillespie, W. H. (1971), "Aggression and Instinct Theory." *Int. J. Psycho-Anal.*, 52:155–160.

49. Green, A. (1972), "Aggression, Femininity, Paranoia and Reality." *Int. J. Psycho-Anal.*, 53:205–211.

50. Greenacre, P. (1949), "A Contribution to the Study of Screen Memories." In *Trauma, Growth and Personality.* New York: Int. Univ. Press, 1969.

51. ——— (1973), "The Primal Scene and the Sense of Reality." *Psychoanal. Quart.*, 42:10–41.

52. Hansen, E. B. (1963), "Probleme bei der Paranoiden Symptombildung." *Psyche*, 17:146–163.

53. Hartmann, H. (1953), "Contribution to the Metapsychology of Schizophrenia." *Psychoanal. Study Child*, 8:177–198.

54. ——— and Kris, E. (1945), "The Genetic Approach in Psychoanalysis." *Psychoanal. Study Child*, 1:11–30.

55. Hofstadter, R. (1965), *The Paranoid Style in American Politics and Other Essays.* New York: Knopf.

56. Jones, E. (1953–57), *The Life and Works of Sigmund Freud.* 3 vol. New York: Basic Books.

57. Kaplan, H. I., and Sadock, B. J. (1971), "The Status of the Paranoid Today: His Diagnosis, Prognosis and Treatment." *Psychiat. Quart.*, 45:528–541.

58. Katan, M. (1950), "Schreber's Hallucinations about the 'Little Men.'" *Int. J. Psycho-Anal.*, 31:32–35.

59. ——— (1950), "Structural Aspects of a Case of Schizophrenia." *Psychoanal. Study Child*, 5:175–211.

60. ——— (1952), "Further Remarks about Schreber's Hallucinations." *Int. J. Psycho-Anal.*, 33.

61. ——— (1954), "The Non-Psychotic Part of the Personality in Schizophrenia." *Int. J. Psycho-Anal.*, 35.

62. ——— (1959), "Schreber's Hereafter: Its Building-Up *(Aufbau)* and Its Downfall." *Psychoanal. Study Child*, 14:314–382.

63. Kitay, P. H. (1963), "Introduction to Symposium on the Schreber Case." *Int. J. Psycho-Anal.*, 44:191–194, 207.

64. Klein, M. (1946), "Notes on Some Schizoid Mechanisms." In *Developments in Psycho-Analysis.* London: Hogarth Press, 1952.

65. ——— (1958), "On the Development of Mental Functioning." *Int. J. Psycho-Anal.*, 39:84–90.

66. Kohut, H. (1960), "Beyond the Bounds of the Basic Rule." *J. Amer. Psychoanal. Assn.*, 3:567–586.

67. ——— (1971), *The Analysis of the Self.* New York: Int. Univ. Press.

68. Kolb, L. C. (1971), *Modern Clinical Psychiatry*. Philadelphia: Saunders.
69. Laffal, J. (1965), *Pathological and Normal Language*. New York: Atherton Press.
70. Levin, S. (1971), "The Depressive Core in Schizophrenia." *Bull. Phila. Assn. Psychoanal.*, 21:219–229.
71. Lewin, B. D. (1968), *The Image and the Past*. New York: Int. Univ. Press.
72. ——— (1971), "Metaphor, Mind and Manikin." *Psychoanal. Quart.*, 40: 6–39.
73. Lidz, T. M. (1968), *The Person: His Development Throughout the Life Cycle*. New York: Basic Books.
74. ———, Fleck, S., and Cornelison, A. (1965), *Schizophrenia and the Family*. New York: Int. Univ. Press.
75. London, N. J. (1973), "An Essay on Psychoanalytic Theory: Two Theories of Schizophrenia." *Int. J. Psycho-Anal.*, 54:169–193.
76. Macalpine, I., and Hunter, R. A. (1955), *Daniel Paul Schreber: Memoirs of My Nervous Illness*. London: Dawson.
77. Mangner, E. (1876), *Dr. D. G. M. Schreber: Ein Kämpfer für Volkserziehung*. Leipzig: Selbstverlag.
78. Mitscherlich, A. (1971), "Psychoanalysis and the Aggression of Large Groups." *Int. J. Psycho-Anal.*, 52:161–168.
79. ——— and Mitscherlich, M. (1969), *Die Unfähigkeit zu Trauern*. Munchen: Piper.
80. Mittelmann, B. (1958), "Psychodynamics of Motility." *Int. J. Psycho-Anal.*, 39.
81. Modlin, H. C. (1963), "Psychodynamics of Paranoid States in Women." *Arch. Gen. Psychiat.*, 8:263–268.
82. Niederland, W. G. (1958), "Early Auditory Experiences, Beating Fantasies, and Primal Scene." *Psychoanal. Study Child*, 13:471–504.
83. ——— (1963), "The Psychopathology and Management and Paranoid States." In *Lectures on Dynamic Psychiatry*, edited by M. Kurian and M. H. Hand. New York: Int. Univ. Press.
84. ——— (1969), "Schreber's Angewunderte Kindheitswelt." *Psyche*, 23:196–223.
85. ——— (1970), "Paranoia: Theory and Therapy. *Psychiat. and Soc. Science Rev.*, 4:2–7.
86. Nunberg, H. (1955), *Principles of Psychoanalysis*. New York: Int. Univ. Press.
87. Nydes, J. (1963), "Schreber, Parricide and Paranoid Masochism." *Int. J. Psycho-Anal.*, 44:208–212.
88. Pao, P. (1972), "Notes on Freud's Theory of Schizophrenia." Lecture delivered at Amer. Psychoanal. Assn. meeting, December, 1972.
89. Politzer, L. M. (1862), "Daniel Gottlieb Moritz Schreber." *Jahrbuch für Kinderheilkunde*, 5.
90. Racamier, P. C., and Chasseguet-Smirgel, J. (1966), "La Révision du Cas Schreber." *Revue Française de Psychoanal.*, 30:3–26.
91. Ritter, A. (1936), "Schreber: Das Bildungssystem eines Arztes." Erlangen: Inaugural Dissertation.
92. Roazen, P. (1969), *Brother Animal*. New York: Knopf.

93. Sachs, O. (1967), "Distinctions between Fantasy and Reality: Elements in Memory and Reconstruction." *Int. J. Psycho-Anal.*, 48:416–423.

94. Schreber, D. G. M. (1839), *Das Buch der Gesundheit.* Leipzig: H. Fries.

95. ——— (1846), *Die Verhütung der Rückgratsverkrümmung oder des Schiefwuchses.* Leipzig: Fleischer.

96. ——— (1852), *Die Eigentümlichkeiten des Kindlichen Organismus in Gesundem und Krankem Zustande.* Leipzig: Fleischer.

97. ——— (1855), *Ärztliche Zimmergymnastik.* Leipzig: Fleischer.

98. ——— (1858), *Kallipaedie oder Erziehung zur Schönheit. . . .* Leipzig: Fleischer.

99. ——— (1859a), *Anthropos: Der Wunderbau des menschlichen Organismus.* Leipzig: Fleischer.

100. ——— (1859b), *Die Planmässige Schärfung der Sinnesorgane.* Leipzig: Fleischer.

101. ——— (1862), *Das Pangymnastikon oder das Ganze Turnsystem an einem Einzigen Geräte. . . .* Leipzig: Fleischer.

102. Schreber, D. P. (1903), *Denkwürdigkeiten eines Nervenkranken.* Leipzig: O. Mutze.

103. Searles, R. (1961), "Sexual Process in Schizophrenia." *Psychiatry, 24;* Supp. 2:87–95.

104. ——— (1961), "The Sources of the Anxiety in Paranoid Schizophrenia." *Brit. J. Med. Psychol.*, 34:129–141.

105. Shengold, L. (1961), "Chekov and Schreber: Vicissitudes of a Certain Kind of Father-Son Relationship." *Int. J. Psycho-Anal.*, 42:431–438.

106. Schilling, K. (1950), "Dr. Schreber und der Schrebergarten." In *Kleingärtner Jahrbuch.* Hamburg: Christen.

107. Sillman, L. R. (1966), "Femininity and Paranoidism." *J. Nerv. and Ment. Dis.*, 143:163–170.

108. Stierlin, H. (1964/65), "Bleuler's Begriff der Schizophrenie im Lichte unserer Heutigen Erfahrungen." *Psyche*, 10:630–642.

109. Sylvester, E. (1959), "Psychological Consequences of Physical Illness in Childhood." *J. Amer. Psychoanal. Assn.*, 7.

110. Swanson, D. W., Bohnert, P. J., and Smith, J. A. (1970), *The Paranoid.* Boston: Little, Brown.

111. Veszy-Wagner, L. (1967), "Zwangsneurose und Latente Homosexualität." *Psyche*, 21:592–615.

112. Volkan, V. D. (1972), "The Linking Objects of Pathological Mourners." *Arch. Gen. Psychiat.*, 27:215–221.

113. Waelder, R. (1951), "The Structure of Paranoid Ideas." *Int. J. Psycho-Anal.*, 32:167–177.

114. Wechsler, M. (1971), "Schizophrenia: Conflict and Deficiency." *Psychoanal. Quart.*, 40:83–99.

115. Zilboorg, G. (1941), *A History of Medical Psychology.* New York: W. W. Norton.

PART III

OTHER ASPECTS OF THE CASE

The study of the Schreber case offers a wide range of personal, clinical, and cultural topics of interest to both the scientist and the lay person. Accordingly, a large number of papers, books, and periodicals in several languages have covered various aspects of the patient's life history, and the publications dealing with it could easily fill many volumes.

As author and editor of this book, I had therefore to select some—by no means all—of those contributions which focused primarily on the intricacies of the case and at the same time added to our understanding of it via extension and further clarification. Other contributions, no less pertinent perhaps, but not of major specific relevance to the problems under consideration, had to be omitted. For reasons of space, some of the papers reprinted in this section were abbreviated and excerpted. I am greatly indebted to the authors for their permission to do so. The papers included in Part III are presented in the chronological order of their original appearance. Chapter 19, "A Note on Soul Murder: Vampire Fantasies," has not previously appeared in print.

14 / Schreber's Delusion of the End of the World[1]

Maurits Katan

More than thirty years ago, Freud inaugurated a new approach to the understanding of the structure of delusions. He used Schreber's Autobiography mainly for the elucidation of two theories: 1, delusion is a defense against homosexuality; 2, delusion is an attempt at restitution.

The same material Freud used can be taken for further investigation. The following is a review of Schreber's basic conflict which led to his idea that the world was lost. Only the function of this idea, namely, the warding off of a danger, will be discussed in this paper. The mechanism, the structure of this idea, or of the delusion in general, will not be considered.

Schreber's illness may be divided into several periods. It started with a prepsychotic phase in which his whole personality was already changed but no psychotic symptoms were present. Schreber stated in his autobiography that after having been appointed to the presidency of the highest court of justice in Saxony, he dreamed that it would be delightful to be a woman submitting to intercourse. After undertaking his new career, he developed a "neurasthenic" hypochondriacal syndrome which exhausted him completely, culminating one night when he was so excited he had six seminal emissions. At this point his psychosis started, in which Professor Flechsig, who was treating him, became his persecutor. Schreber's principal delusion was that Flechsig had interfered with the order of things in the universe. According to "the order of things," everybody's nerves would, after death, go through a process of purification which would last up to thousands of years. The purified nerves would become part of the "forecourts of heaven" and there attain a state of bliss. The forecourts of heaven he considered to be a part of God, and God himself floated above them. God got his energy from these forecourts of heaven and this enabled Him to create things on earth so that an eternal circle was developed.

Under certain circumstances, if someone got into a state of excitement God could be attracted by this man and His power would be jeopardized; but the "order of things" provided against this contingency. God would then destroy mankind, sparing only the best man on earth, who, after being transformed

[1] Reprinted from *The Psychoanalytic Quarterly*, Vol. 18, No. 1 (January, 1949), with the author's permission.

into a woman, would become the wife of God. This feminized man would then bring forth children who would be the source of a new mankind. This would still be in accordance with the "order of things."

Schreber had now got into such a state of excitement that he attracted God. Flechsig got knowledge of it and started to abuse this power for his own purposes. The soul of Flechsig went up to heaven without being dead and without passing through the process of purification. There he caught and gained control of the rays of God, and used them for his own purposes. At first God did not want this, but after a little while He yielded to it. In this way Flechsig became the leader of a conspiracy against Schreber. Several times Flechsig attempted to murder Schreber's soul. (The official censor deleted from the published Autobiography all the remarks attributed to Flechsig concerning this murder of Schreber's soul, so we do not know what they were; the only information which we have is that Schreber compared himself with Faust in that he would get earthly advantages in exchange for his soul.) He successfully warded off all these attacks on his soul. Still, these attempts were against "the order of things" and destroyed the plan of the wonderful structure in the hereafter. It was no longer possible for Schreber or for any human being to gain bliss in the hereafter, because the nerves of no human being could any longer be purified after death; therefore God lost the supply of energy from the earth. By this loss God felt himself threatened and tried in vain to abandon Schreber. A conflict arose between Schreber and God through the interference of Flechsig. This conflict with God caused Schreber to get terrible visions of the destruction of the world. Voices told him that the world was lost and, after a while, he was convinced that the world no longer existed. He was the only remaining living being in the world, and he saw his fellow men as people placed there by a miracle for only a short period of time.

Although he tried several times to get rid of Flechsig, who came between God and himself, Schreber did not succeed in doing away with him. Many important changes in Schreber's symptomatology took place at this time. Gradually he became more and more aware of feminine traits in his body. After two years he no longer could resist the transformation which took place in his body and he made up his mind that he could no longer resist the idea of emasculation; that his change into a woman would be in the interest of "the order of things." After more than two hundred years the change of his body into that of a woman would be completed and he would become the wife of God. Some days after Schreber had accepted this transformation, he became aware of the fact that physical reality had not altered, although a psychological change had taken place.

With the feminine rôle came the obligation to keep himself in a state of feminine excitement, otherwise God would abandon him. In reaching this goal, he imagined himself to be man and woman in one person, having intercourse together. He supported this by certain acts, such as embracing himself, but he remarked that such actions were not to be regarded as lascivious and that any thought of masturbation should be excluded. He explained it from the point of being a woman, so that after the acceptance of his transformation he masturbated almost continuously with fantasies that he was a woman having intercourse. We know from Schreber's prepsychotic phase that he was then also possessed by the wish to be a woman; that this excited him so much, he was hypersensitive to any stimulation from men around him; that at the end of his prepsychotic phase, this excitement caused no less than six emissions in one night.

Before we can discuss the meaning of the end of the world, we have to consider Schreber's delusions about the wonderful structure of the hereafter, and what the murder of his soul meant. Even if the censor had not deleted Schreber's statements about this last subject, it is questionable that our knowledge about it would have been greatly enlarged. In the entire book no remark is made about it. Fortunately, a change of hospital residence brought us the desired information. After his psychosis had lasted for more than half a year, he was removed from the University Clinic to another hospital, for reasons which are easily understood. When this took place, Flechsig's soul split itself into forty or sixty parts, and spread all over heaven so that it was impossible for the rays of God to reach Schreber directly. As if this were not enough, there appeared in heaven another soul which also split itself into twenty or thirty parts. This was the soul of the chief male nurse at the new institution to whom Schreber gave the name von W because he believed this attendant to be his former neighbor, von W.

Voices told Schreber that von W accused him of masturbation, which Schreber denied. Our interpretation is that this was an affirmation of the fact that the presence of von W stimulated him to masturbate with fantasies about him. Schreber's denial means that he had succeeded in warding off this temptation to masturbate.

Schreber reveals how he came to believe von W got this influence. Flechsig wanted to catch the rays of God to use them for his own purposes. As Schreber was the focus of these rays, because he attracted them to himself, Flechsig needed his presence as a bait. But after Schreber's removal to another clinic, a separation took place between Flechsig and Schreber. Flechsig's soul now called for help from the soul of von W because von W, in the new institution, had the power over Schreber's body; thus it becomes clear that Flechsig exercised the same influence upon Schreber as von W did; therefore Flechsig and all his assistants excited Schreber so much that he could hardly resist the temptation to masturbate.

In exchange for his soul, earthly advantages would be bestowed upon him. These advantages become identical with permission to masturbate with homosexual fantasies about Flechsig; hence, the murder of the soul means yielding to the temptation aroused by Flechsig to masturbate with thoughts about him. But he successfully warded off these "attacks."

Freud's interpretation of the plan about the wonderful structure of the hereafter, which was in accordance with "the order of things," was that the forecourts of heaven mean femininity. This is corroborated by Schreber's statement that the souls, after their purification, become part of the forecourts of heaven and get into a state of feminine bliss by seeing God, indicating that purification means castration, and that men in the hereafter would be transformed into women. God floating over the forecourts of heaven is a symbol of intercourse. Schreber believed, then, that he would be transformed into a woman in the hereafter and as such enjoy intercourse with God. Somewhere else Schreber mentioned that men are the images of God. Given Schreber's extreme narcissism we conclude that, in his delusions, God is Schreber's image, a reflection of his bisexuality.

To better understand the plan about the wonderful structure in the hereafter, let us re-examine Schreber's state after he had accepted the idea of being transformed into a woman. He had the compulsion to masturbate continuously, playing the rôles of man and woman in one, and exhibiting feminine voluptuousness to attract God. A basic masturbatory fantasy is at work in all periods of his illness.

Originally, in his prepsychotic state, he was disturbed by homosexual excitement which culminated in six emissions (masturbatory equivalents) in a single night. Following this he lost hold on reality and his psychosis began.

It becomes clear from Schreber's ideas about the hereafter that in his psychosis he had hoped to ward off masturbation during his lifetime. He expected that in the hereafter his long suppressed wish for femininity would be fulfilled. If he could suppress this desire and the resulting masturbation the rest of his life, he would in the hereafter be completely compensated for his sacrifices. This delusional plan never functioned, for Flechsig and the group around him, by their mere presence, excited him so much.

At this point, ideas of the end of the world entered into his system of delusions. He was terrified by the thought of yielding to the temptation of masturbation aroused by Flechsig. This would mean that he would accept the earthly advantages and lose his soul. The loss of his soul would mean that he would have to give up forever the hope of contact with God. Had that happened, he would have maintained "the world," that is, masturbation involving Flechsig, and would forever have lost God. Only one outlet remained open to him: as contact with God in the hereafter became impossible, he could strive for the possibility of a union with God during his lifetime. This goal was to be attained only by suppressing masturbation; he had to defend his soul and reject the temptation, stimulated by Flechsig, to masturbate.

Herein we find the origin of the delusion that the world was lost. As a corollary to this delusion, Schreber thought that Flechsig and his assistants did not exist in reality but were miraculously put there for a short period. This was a defense against the homosexual attraction which the men surrounding him exerted upon him. The period which followed, until Schreber's transformation, shows us his flight from the dangers arising from his love for Flechsig. This conflict is expressed in numerous persecutory and hypochondriacal delusions, various hallucinations and a catatonic state.

At last victory was his. He had succeeded in obtaining the much desired contact with God by the acceptance of his change into a woman. The process that made this change possible is revealed by the conspicuous fact that from that point on Schreber was able to masturbate: God forced him to do it, otherwise He would leave him; furthermore, this masturbation had a peculiar characteristic. Schreber described it as being of a gentle, pleasant nature. Genital sensations were lacking, so there were no phenomena like erection or emission. We conclude that at the moment he yielded to accepting the feminine rôle, he had at last succeeded in suppressing his masculine genital functioning whenever he was sexually excited. Before he had reached that point his genitals threatened to react whenever his sexuality was aroused. The mastery of his genital functions made possible the acceptance of the feminine rôle.

After this achievement Flechsig and the others were no longer a great danger to him, now that he did not have to fear genital reactions to homosexual stimulations. That is the reason why, in relation to his acceptance of his future transformation, it became apparent that the world was still there.

The contrasting influences which God and Flechsig exerted on Schreber are the projection of the conflicting attachments to God and to Flechsig. Both are of a homosexual nature. The ultimate meaning of the attachment to Flechsig is the embodiment of a form of masturbation in which the reaction of the penis is included. This form is forbidden, in contrast to the other in which the penis does not share in the excitement, and which is symbolized by the attachment to God.

The delusion that the world is lost is limited to a certain period; no central significance can be attached to it. As long as Schreber was not able to master his genital functioning, he needed this delusion to help ward off this danger.

15 / Schreber's Hereafter: Its Building-Up (Aufbau) and Its Downfall[1]

Maurits Katan

INTRODUCTION

Schreber's *Denkwürdigkeiten* has a peculiar structure. He wrote the main portion of the book between February and September 1900. The book begins with a Preface dated December 1902, an Open Letter to Flechsig dated March 1903, and an Introduction which obviously was written in February 1900. Because the Preface and the Open Letter were written so much later, a discussion of them can take place only after we have studied the entire book.

The book itself may be divided into three parts. In this article I shall deal only with the first part, which consists of a brief introduction and three chapters, but the last of these three chapters has been deleted by the censor. In the fourth chapter Schreber finally begins with a chronological account of his illness, which he follows for the remainder of the book.

One may regard this first part as an informative account of how Schreber became ill. The first chapter, which he entitles "God and Immortality," pictures the organization of the hereafter. The second chapter deals with the opposing force which caused the hereafter eventually to lose its organization.

Schreber tells in his Introduction why he wrote the autobiography of his illness. In the beginning of 1900 he was in the midst of a struggle to regain his freedom after he had been hospitalized for more than six years. At that time he still had the intention of returning to his wife, and the original and primary aim of writing the story of his illness was to inform his wife of his experiences and religious ideas. During his occupation with this work, he felt compelled to seek publication in order to enlighten humanity.

Schreber's unconscious motives for writing and publishing the autobiography of his illness can be made clear only by the analysis of his illness. Thus I cannot enter into a discussion of his motives. I will make use of some of the introductory material because, from the practical point of view, this belongs to the first chapter.

[1] This article is the first part of Dr. Katan's paper, reprinted from *The Psychoanalytic Study of the Child*, Vol. 14 (1959), with the author's permission.

127

I. GOD AND IMMORTALITY

Our first step is to become acquainted with the order of the world. In Chapter I, "God and Immortality," Schreber introduces us to this order by telling us that the souls of human beings are contained in the nerves of their bodies. All psychic life takes place through the nerves. Thus, for instance, the nerves react with pleasure and displeasure to stimuli from the outside. They are able to retain memories, to cause actions, to perform intellectual functions, etc. Each single intellect nerve represents the total psychic individuality of the human being, that is, contains all the memories, and the number of these intellect nerves determines only how long certain memories are retained. In the nerves, too, human development has its origin. Semen, for instance, contains the nerve of the father, the nerve which unites with the nerve of the mother to form a new unit. In this connection let me repeat the following sentences from the Introduction, which are noteworthy: "Nobody will say that God as a creature provided with human genitals has had intercourse with the woman from whose lap came Jesus Christ" (p. 3). "Something similar to the conception Jesu Christi by an immaculate virgin, i.e., a woman who has never had intercourse with a man, has occurred in my body." Schreber felt himself impregnated by the divine nerves, these nerves corresponding to male semen (p. 4).

During life the human being is body and soul together. But with the death of the body, the nerves become unconscious, a state which we call death and which already has sleep as its example. Therefore, the soul is not really extinguished but passes through a state of hibernation, from which it can be awakened to new life (p. 7).

God himself is only nerve, not body. God is therefore closely related to the human soul but far superior to it in that he contains an unlimited number of nerves and is eternal. God possesses the ability to create things on earth through the nerves, those nerves which travel from God to earth being called rays.

A close relationship exists between God and the starry sky and sun. Schreber cannot decide whether God and the world of stars and sun are one, or whether the stars and sun are merely stations which God uses in creating his wonders on earth. For instance, Schreber states that for years the sun has spoken to him in human words and has manifested itself in this way as a living creature, or perhaps as an organ of a still higher creature behind it. The sun is therefore the instrument nearest to earth through which God's will expresses itself (p. 9).

The sun is also God's eye. Through the light of the sun and stars, God sees everything on earth. He enjoys what he sees there as products of his own creation, similar to the human being who finds pleasure in the labor of his hands or in the creations of his mind.

As a rule, God does not interfere in human lives. Yet it is possible, according to the order of the world, that God on very rare occasions communicates with an individual of exceptional talent. This was called by the voices who talked to Schreber "taking nerve attachment to somebody" in order to bestow graces upon that person through some fertile thoughts and ideas about the hereafter (namely, in the dream). There is danger involved in such communication between God and man, for if the nerves of *living* persons in communication with God *become greatly excited,* they exert such a strong attraction upon God's nerves that the latter cannot free themselves, and God's own existence is then threatened. Thus a development of such "nerve attachment" was not permitted to become a rule. Schreber explains in a footnote which he added some years later (November 1902) that the power of the attraction should not be considered as being purely mechanical in nature, for the rays are living beings. Therefore, the origin of this power is similar to a psychological force. The relation is comparable to the one of which Goethe sings in *Der Fischer:* "Halfway she pulled him, halfway he let himself sink" (p. 11).[2]

Regular communication between God and human souls takes place only after death. God may approach a cadaver without any danger to himself; then, through the power of the rays, God draws the nerves from the body up to himself and, by this process, awakens them to a new heavenly life. The self-awareness of the nerves has not been lost but has merely been lying dormant and now returns under the influence of the rays. The nerves then undergo a process of purification in order to become part of the forecourts of heaven.[3] Once this state is attained, they will enter into a state of bliss. This process of purification lasts shorter or longer according to the individual structure, and eventually these nerves pass through certain interim phases as a means of preparation. God can use only the pure human nerves, for it is their fate finally to become to a certain degree, as forecourts of heaven, a part of God. The nerves of immoral people are black, but the morally pure have white nerves. Practically every nerve must undergo this process of purification because every human being during his existence on earth has committed some sins. It is impossible for Schreber to describe accurately the process of purification, although in this respect he has obtained many valuable hints. It seems that the souls, when they undergo the process of purification, feel as if they were performing a disagreeable task or as if they perhaps were enduring a subterranean stay fraught with discontent, although such a stay is a necessary part of the gradual approach to purification.

"Whoever in this connection wants to apply the expression of punishment may in a certain sense be justified, yet in contradistinction to the human

---

[2] *"Halb zog sie ihn, halb sank er hin."*

[3] In a footnote, Schreber mentions that the expression "forecourts of heaven" was not invented by him, but, like so many other expressions (all of which he has put in quotation marks, such as "fleetingly made up men" or "Dream-life"), is used by the voices. *He would never by himself have arrived at such expressions* and he has never heard them used by other people. They are partly of a scientific and more especially of a medical nature, and Schreber is not even informed whether they are known to human science.

concept of punishment, one should keep in mind that the aim was not to inflict something bad, but only to create a necessary condition for purification. In this way the usual ideas of hell, hell-fire, and so forth, of most religions may find their explanation, but these in part have also to be set right."

During this process of purification, the nerves learn the so-called ground-language, which is the language spoken by God himself. This ground-language is "a somewhat old-fashioned but nevertheless powerful German which is especially characterized by its great wealth of euphemisms." For instance, in the ground-language a number of words mean the reverse: "reward" means "punishment," "poison" means "food," "juice" means "poison," "unsacred" means "sacred," etc.

God himself was called "in consideration of the one who is and will be"—a roundabout expression for eternity—and was addressed as "Eternal Majesty yours faithfully obedient." The purification was called "test"; souls that had not yet gone through the process of purification were not given the name "untested souls," as one might expect, but, in accordance with the tendency to euphemisms, exactly the reverse, "tested souls."

The souls that were in the process of purification were called by names according to various gradations: satans, devils, help-devils, upper devils, and ground devils, the last expression seeming to point to an existence underground. The devils, etc., when they appeared in the role of "men fleetingly made up," had a peculiar color (like beet-red) and a peculiar, repulsive odor, as Schreber noticed in Dr. Pierson's institution. Among others, he saw there Mr. von W, who as a devil had a peculiar red face and red hands. This von W, as we shall see, was later to play a very important role in Schreber's life.

Schreber had heard that Judas Iscariot, because of his betrayal of Jesus Christ, had been a ground devil. Yet contrary to what the Christian religion teaches, the devils were not a force antagonistic to God, but in general were already very God-fearing and were still only in the process of purification.

The fact that God made use of the German language in the form of the so-called "ground-language" should not be construed as meaning that only Germans could become blessed. It might be that God's chosen people, as those who at the time were most outstanding in a moral sense, were successively the Jews, the Persians (these to a very special degree), the Graeco-Romans, and finally the Germans.

After becoming completely purified, the souls ascend to heaven and enter there into a state of bliss. While in this state, they experience uninterrupted enjoyment in beholding God (p. 16). The idea of eternally doing nothing is unbearable to human beings. But the souls are something other than men. The continuous wallowing in pleasure and simultaneous basking in memories of their human past afford the souls the highest satisfaction. The souls, with the help of the rays, are able to keep informed about their relatives and friends on earth. Yet the idea should be rejected that the souls' own happiness could be disturbed by the observation that their relatives who are still alive may be in a very unfortunate situation. For although the souls may keep memories of the past, new impressions which they receive in their new state as souls are retained by them for only a brief period. This is the natural forgetfulness of the souls, who want to get rid of new, unfavorable impressions as soon as possible.

Masculine bliss is of a higher order than feminine bliss; the latter consists mainly of uninterrupted feelings of voluptuousness (p. 18). Through the process of purification, the souls lose consciousness of their identity, some much sooner than others. The souls of great men—Goethe and Bismarck, for instance—may perhaps maintain awareness of their identity for hundreds of years, whereas the souls of children will lose it very soon. An eternal, continuous consciousness of having been this or that man was not the fate of any human soul. Rather it was the fate of all souls, melted together with one another, to be finally dissolved in higher unities, and in this state to feel themselves only still parts of God (forecourts of heaven).

This did not mean an actual annihilation, but living on with another consciousness. In this respect, souls had an eternal continuation. In the long run, a soul could have no interest in remembering who he had been, when already many generations that came after him had also died, and it might even be that the nation to which he had belonged had passed out of existence, too. In this connection Schreber became acquainted with rays—i.e., groups of blessed human souls who had been promoted to higher unities—of the old Jewry (Jehova rays), Persians (Zoroaster rays), and Germans (Thor and Odin rays). They had lost their past identity completely.

As happens so frequently, Schreber gives a most valuable comment, not in the text but as a footnote: "The aforementioned description in relation to the 'forecourts of heaven' perhaps yields simultaneously a suspicion in regard to the eternal round of things, upon which the order of the world is based. When God creates something, he expends to a certain extent a part of himself, or gives a different shape to a part of his nerves. The loss which apparently is developed through this process is again compensated for when the nerves of the deceased, whose bodily maintenance during their earthly lives was provided for by the things which were created in addition, after hundreds and thousands of years, once they [the nerves] have become blessed, as 'forecourts of heaven' accrue again to him [God]."

God himself floats above the forecourts of heaven. These forecourts are called the "front realms of God" in contradistinction to the "back realms of God," which is the name for God himself. These "back realms" are divided into an upper and a lower god; the former is called Ormuzd, the latter Ahriman (p. 19). Schreber does not have anything else to say about this division into two gods, other than that the lower god preferred the people who belonged to what was originally the brunette race (the Semites), and the upper god felt himself drawn more to the people of what was originally the blond race (the Arians). The names Ormuzd and Ahriman, Schreber heard for the first time in July 1894, after having been a week in the "Sonnen-stein." The fact that the names of the two gods were taken from the Persian gods led Schreber to believe that the old Persians were to a very high degree God's chosen people, i.e., a people of very special morality. "The name Ahriman, by the way, occurs also, for instance, in Lord Byron's Manfred in connection with a murder of a soul" (p. 20).

"The aforementioned picture of the nature of God and the continuation of the human soul after death deviates in many respects not unmarkedly from the ideas of the Christian religion on these matters. An all-knowing and ever-present God, in the sense that God gazed *steadily* into the interior of every living man, would observe any rise of feeling of his nerves, also at any given moment would test man's innermost core, indeed did not exist." This God does not need to, because, when he sees the nerves of the deceased, they con-tain all the impressions which they received when alive, and from this ob-servation, God is able to judge the souls. Also, there is no sign of that grue-someness sometimes so predominant in the Christian religion and even more so in other religions. Therefore the whole of the world order impresses Schreber as a "wonderful building-up" incomparably more sublime than all other ideas which people have formed during the ages about their relation to God.

A footnote gives more information about the origin of the "wonderful building-up" [*der "wundervolle Aufbau"*]. "Again an expression which is not invented by me. I would have, of course, in the thought- or nerve-language, which will be mentioned later, spoken of *wonderful organization*, whereupon the expression 'wonderful building-up'[4] was prompted to me from the outside."

INTERPRETATION

A. The Meaning of the Delusions

Indeed, the picture of the hereafter as Schreber reveals it to us must have been to him most attractive. Our attention is immediately drawn to the rich reward which awaits everyone in the hereafter: after having passed through purgatory, the souls will attain a state of bliss. This purgatory lacks any of the characteristics of a punishment; it is merely a necessary transitional phase in order to reach one's destination of being taken up into the forecourts of heaven, which are already a part of God. The souls are in a state of con-

[4] The translation of *"Aufbau"* caused me (M. Katan) great difficulty. "Structure," used by Strachey, did not seem to me adequate, being too foreign, for the ground-language threw out even *"Organisation"* and took *"Aufbau"* instead. "Built-up" would perhaps be the correct word if this did not already have a completely different connotation in English.

tinual pleasure; disagreeable impressions, in case any should appear, especially about living relatives in distress, are almost immediately forgotten, and punishment does not exist.

What other conclusion can we draw than that the souls are living according to the unlimited pleasure principle? Obviously Schreber has reserved a part of himself, which never had a chance to attain satisfaction during his lifetime, for compensation in the hereafter, where it may indulge itself in limitless pleasure. Even the devils seem to be tame; instead of being rebellious, they are to a great extent God-fearing. We understand fully that Schreber prefers this picture of the hereafter to any other professed by official religions. All harshness or gruesomeness seems to be absent from the wonderful structure.

Yet, upon closer consideration, the area of enjoyment in the hereafter has a rather narrow field of operation, the main avenue being the beholding of God. Next, it strikes us that God's existence is not at all as secure as one might expect. God's existence is endangered if he comes under an exceptional attraction by a living human being. Once our suspicion is aroused, we must admit that there is also something doubtful about the concept of the lack of punishment and its relation to the devils. Reviewing the facts that devils are those souls which must submit to disagreeable tasks and that some of them lead a subterranean existence, we conclude, if appearances do not deceive us, that they are forced to do penance. For instance, Judas Iscariot, because of his betrayal of Jesus Christ, was a ground devil. In other aspects, such as their detectability by color and odor, the devils seem to have retained certain characteristics of the Devil as we know him.

Our next question is: why does it take certain souls so long to lose their identity, as if they resisted giving up a cherished possession? For it would seem to us that if they want so much to become a part of the forecourts of heaven, keeping their identity cannot be of much use to them.

Another point: in the hereafter, enjoyment in beholding God seems to be a precarious thing. If God's own existence can be endangered, then the soul's enjoyment is threatened at the same time. Surely we are required to make a much more detailed examination if we want to arrive at a better understanding.

Let us begin by considering Schreber's statement that a strong similarity exists between God and the human soul, God surpassing the human soul only because he is limitless and eternal. Obviously Schreber has himself in mind as an example of the human soul. We may therefore expect that Schreber's god will bear a resemblance to Schreber's conception of his own personality (see also Katan, 1949).

Next, we are reminded of the eternal round. The souls accrue to God as "forecourts of heaven" and are then in a state of bliss beholding the back realms. The latter expend a part of themselves in the form of rays, which do creative work on earth. From these creations on earth, in turn, comes the material from which the forecourts of heaven are replenished. Thus a system of maintenance of energy is established in the hereafter.

In order to study this eternal round, let us concentrate on the organ(s) from which the rays emanate. The sun and stars play an important part in the relationship between God and the earth. Although Schreber leaves open the possibility that God is identical with the sun and stars, he nevertheless seems to be inclined to consider the sun God's main organ. Here it should be recalled from Schreber's description that the rays (i.e., nerves emanating from the sun) possess also the characteristic of being spermatozoa. This characteristic is emphasized by Schreber when he remarks that God has no human genitals but is nevertheless able to impregnate him (Schreber) through the rays, a process similar to the Immaculate Conception[5] (pp. 3–4).

It therefore becomes clear that to Schreber the sun and stars represent God's masculine genitals, and the "back realms of God" mean masculinity. The sun has other attributes, being also God's eye whereby he derives enjoyment from beholding the wonders which he has created on earth. We will take up this point shortly.

Let us next clarify the meaning of the "forecourts of heaven." These forecourts constitute the front part of God; they are maintained by those souls who have been purified. These souls are in a state of bliss, which consists of *uninterrupted* enjoyment in beholding God (p. 16). Schreber also remarks that *female* feelings of voluptuousness are characterized by being *uninterrupted* (p. 18). We may therefore conclude that the purified souls enjoy feelings of feminine voluptuousness and that the forecourts are *identical with femininity*.

Here Freud has already shown us the direction, for in still another way he has interpreted the forecourts as being feminine. The "wondered" ("speaking") birds, according to Freud's beautiful deduction (1911, p. 36), represented girls. Since Schreber described these birds as being remnants of the forecourts of heaven, it is clear that the forecourts, too, must be feminine. Thus we may consider our interpretation as a supplement to Freud's.

This interpretation of the forecourts of heaven enables us to understand the meaning of the *process of purification*. Here we find the idea that the souls who live on after the body dies are transformed by purification into females. In this process, the souls lose their identity. Thus we may equate identity with masculinity. As has already been stated, the souls of very outstanding persons, such as Goethe and Bismarck, may retain their identity ($=$ masculinity) for a long time, but in the end even these souls cannot escape transformation into women.[6]

[5] The identification with "Maria" should here be noted.

[6] Niederland (1951) defends the opinion that Schreber became ill in order to withdraw from the powerful influence of Bismarck. Bismarck is mentioned by Schreber *only once*. I do not think there is any reason to assume—not even in view of Schreber's

It seems to me that certain traits of the "ground-language" show characteristics similar to those of the process of purification. The "ground-language" is a somewhat old-fashioned but nevertheless powerful German. It strikes the observer that any word containing a hint of some foreign origin is dropped and exchanged for a purer German expression. For example, Schreber would have spoken of the *wonderful organization* to indicate the structure of the hereafter, had not "wonderful building-up" been prompted to him from the outside. Accordingly we are led to conclude that the "ground-language" as such has been combed by the process of purification. This conclusion finds particular support in the fact that the souls, when they undergo purification, learn this so-called "ground-language." Thus this language expresses the aim of purification.

We find this also stressed by another conspicuous feature of the "ground-language," namely, the use of euphemisms. As an example, Schreber mentions a number of words whose meanings have been changed into the reverse: "reward" means "punishment," "poison" means "food," "juice" means "poison," "unsacred" means "sacred." Those souls that are in the process of purification are called "tested souls" and not "untested souls."

We are struck by the fact that the reversal of meaning of certain words in the "ground-language" coincides with the process which also had as its aim a turning around into the opposite, namely, the transformation from a man into a woman. Therefore it is now easy to say that this important transformation showed its influence by bringing about the reversal of meaning of a number of words. Accordingly we may venture our opinion that the "ground-language" contains a beautiful example of displacement of the process of purification.

For the time being, let us leave this interesting subject of purification and ask what will happen to Schreber's discarded masculinity. Although Schreber does not mention it, it is clear that the accrual of Schreber's femininity to the forecourts of heaven is not sufficient to explain the eternal round from an economical point of view. For in this way no energy derived from the souls would be transmitted to the back realms of God. This gap in our understanding is immediately closed by the conclusion that the back realms of God are replenished by the masculine part of the nerves of the deceased. The back realms of God are the projection of Schreber's own lost masculinity. Since Schreber conceives of the sun and stars as the masculine parts of God, we may conclude that these heavenly bodies symbolize Schreber's own masculine

---

previous candidacy for the *Reichstag,* during which period he broke down for the first time—that Bismarck had anything to do with Schreber's illness. On the contrary, far from being a frightening figure, Bismarck, who is mentioned in the same breath with Goethe, is highly admired by Schreber for his strong masculinity and does not contain any persecutory features.

Editor's note: With regard to Bismarck's role in the *Kulturkampf* situation as it affected Schreber, see my article "Margraves of Tuscany and Tasmania," pp. 85ff.

genitals. Thus we see that in the hereafter Schreber's masculine and feminine components will be completely separated from each other and will constitute the back and front realms of God.[7]

We are now ready to examine the relationship between the forecourts of heaven (the front realms of God) and God himself (the back realms of God). The picture of God floating above the forecourts is symbolic of sexual intercourse (Katan, 1949).

In his design of the hereafter, Schreber has grown enormously in power: he has promoted himself to God. His god is a very conspicuous one: he consists of a male and a female component, and both are projections of Schreber's own bisexual valencies (Katan, 1949). Schreber has shown awareness of this fact by saying that God is related to the human soul. In his extensions, however, he surpasses the human soul, for the number of God's nerves are endless and eternal. Nevertheless, by externalizing the masculine part, Schreber feels himself identical with only the female part. These two parts are united in intercourse.

Let us look more closely at this strange god. Indeed, it is a picture of self-sufficiency, and we may conclude that Schreber saw in it a fulfilled masturbatory ideal of extreme narcissistic character. The two valencies of his bisexuality will be united in the act of masturbation, in the hereafter.

At this point a host of questions arise. Why could this ideal be fulfilled only in the hereafter and not during Schreber's lifetime? Why did Schreber have to identify himself with femininity? Why was the eternal round necessary, and why did scoptophilic tendencies play such a major role? Indeed, there are certain peculiarities which cannot at first sight be reconciled with an idealistic satisfaction in the hereafter.

Let us start with the problem of why Schreber could become only the feminine part of this bisexual God. Why could he not keep his masculine habitus? We have a good reason for posing this question, for Schreber states explicitly, "Masculine bliss is of a higher order than feminine bliss," without stipulating any further what this higher order consists of. Yet from his statement, we may conclude his preference for masculine bliss. We have already met with a similar symptom: outstanding men like Bismarck and Goethe would preserve their identity (= masculinity) much longer than anybody else. Thus we gain the conviction that even if Schreber's femininity was not used as a defense but arose from a strong, genuine need, there still remained a great reluctance to surrender his masculinity. Once this point has become clear, it is not difficult to find the traces of a tenacious struggle against castration in his delusional concept of God.

Let us turn to the eternal round which forms the basis of the world order.

[7] Since we know that Schreber's "ground-language" was a purified German in which all words having in them anything of a foreign extraction were abolished, it does not seem correct to translate *"die vorderen und hinteren Gottesreiche"* as "the anterior and posterior realms of God."

When God creates something on earth, he does this from his own energy, that is, he gives up a part of himself. But this apparent loss is compensated for, after hundreds or thousands of years, when the souls of the deceased, after having been purified, accrue to him again as forecourts of heaven. Without even going into further detail, we can see in "this principle of the maintenance of energy" that God, in the hereafter, is trying to protect himself against the danger of castration.

What does God create on earth? The loss which God suffers through his creative productivity is restored, for the nerves of the deceased, once they have become blessed as forecourts of heaven, accrue again to God after a very long time. Although Schreber does not say so explicitly, we may conclude from the description that God creates human beings. The things which God has made in addition (*die übrigen erschaffenen Dinge*) serve the purpose of taking care of the body as long as human beings are alive. This peculiar wording points again to a conclusion: God creates people and the things to keep people alive. Thus the masturbatory fantasy about the hereafter which forms the content of the delusion leads to the production of children, and in this way Schreber hopes to compensate himself in the hereafter for the lack of children during his lifetime.

Yet there is a much more pressing motive for creating children than the compensatory one. The children (human beings) are the necessary link in the chain with which Schreber safeguards his masculinity in the hereafter. As we have seen, the loss is canceled: the lost nerves accrue to God again. Our surprising conclusion is that in the hereafter Schreber, i.e., God, will produce children all by himself in order to find protection against castration.

The process by which the feminine forecourts of heaven participate in the creation of children remains obscure. Schreber states only that God, i.e., the masculine part, when he creates something on earth, expends to a certain extent a part of himself or gives a different shape to a part of his nerves. It is possible that the infantile fantasy of the child being made from a piece of the father's penis is partially responsible for the content of this delusion. Anyhow, once men die, their souls will be split in the hereafter into a feminine and a masculine part again, and thus the eternal round will remain unbroken; that is, the castration danger in the hereafter is successfully warded off.

We can find further evidence of the defense against castration in the hereafter by pointing to the prominence of the scoptophilic tendencies of God, a subject to which we have so far not given any attention. Not only do the souls in the forecourts of heaven (i.e., the front realms of God) experience their uninterrupted voluptuous feelings in beholding God, but also God (i.e., the back realms) enjoys looking at the things which he has created. Both scoptophilic tendencies seem to me to be of a strong supportive nature in the defense against the danger of castration. What better proof can be possible that nothing is lost than uninterruptedly perceiving that the threatened object is still present and unharmed? For this is, in fact, the case. When God looks at his own creations, a part of his pleasure may be based upon the reassurance that what he has surrendered is not lost but will be found again, transformed into another form. The same is true of feminine bliss. The discarded masculinity has returned in its projected form of the back realms; as such, it is visible, without any interruption, to the souls of the forecourts of heaven —a scoptophilic process which leads to a state of bliss.

Finally, after taking note of these various trends, we come to the conclusion that Schreber's greatest concern about the hereafter was how he could protect himself against castration. Even so, notwithstanding the delusional *projection* of his masculinity, Schreber was not at all sure that his psychotic defense would be sufficient to guarantee an undisturbed hereafter. The attraction exerted by a living human being might endanger God's existence, and the order of the world contained certain provisions to cope with such a situation in case it should arise. From the entire picture, we form the idea that the immortality of the soul at which Schreber aimed was threatened by forces which Schreber had not yet revealed. Connected with this problem is, without any doubt, the fact that although Schreber professed masculine bliss to be of a higher order than feminine bliss, he was not yet striving after masculine bliss in the hereafter. We might increase our understanding if we compare the delusion of the hereafter with certain situations which Schreber went through before he became psychotic in the proper sense.

For this purpose let us turn to Schreber's prepsychotic phase (Katan, 1953). We are struck by the similarity between Schreber's delusion of the hereafter and his prepsychotic ideas. After his appointment as *Senatspräsident,* but before he betrayed any signs of illness, Schreber dreamed on several occasions that his former illness had returned. It was a great relief, upon awakening, to find that these dreams were not true. One morning, in a state between sleeping and waking, it also occurred to him how pleasant it would be to be a woman submitting to intercourse.

We may ask whether Schreber's desire to be a woman submitting to intercourse became conscious because it was a defense (for instance, against a danger arising from oedipal demands) or whether this idea resulted from an unconscious desire, which had no relation to the oedipus complex, breaking through to consciousness. Schreber's dreams and the well-known course which his illness took leave us in no doubt that his desire to be a woman was not a defense. His entire prepsychotic period was marked by the struggle against this desire. In my article on Schreber's prepsychotic phase (1953), I have explained that these dreams expressed the hope that he would be able to master the urge toward femininity so that he would not have to become psychotic in order to cope with this urge. Schreber's hope was not fulfilled. We can follow his struggle against this trend until the latter forced the ego to sever relations with reality. This happened immediately after the night when Schreber's excitement resulting from the feminine wish discharged itself in a large number of pollutions.

In this final stage of Schreber's prepsychotic period, the ego could no longer rely upon sufficiently strong oedipal relationships for a widespread contact with reality. On the one hand, the ego had to ward off the wish to be a woman for fear of losing its masculinity. *If the wish to be a woman were to be expressed by a genital orgasm, it would mean that this feminine wish would be fulfilled, and the genital orgasm would therefore mean the annihilation of his penis.* On the other hand, the ego, in order to remain in contact with reality, also needed the use of this urge toward femininity, for this urge exerted a strong pressure to maintain contact with reality, and in this respect ego and urge had a common aim. Thus the ego was cornered and found itself in an impossible situation: orgasm would mean castration, and orgasm could be warded off only by abandoning the drive toward femininity; yet for its contact with reality, the ego needed this drive.

As a rule, the outcome of this struggle is such that the ego does not wait until it is overwhelmed by sexual excitement but abandons contact with reality in advance of the occurrence of this excitement. This was not true of Schreber, however. In his case, the urge toward femininity finally forced its way to expression in a genital orgasm during sleep, and then for the remainder of the night the gates were down. We see on that particular night how very much the ego was on the side of the instinct. It is quite possible that someone else, in order to stay in command of the situation, would have refrained from sleeping for the remainder of the night. Yet Schreber's ego was unable to do so. This inability to stay awake gives us reason to wonder. Schreber's main concern from the time of onset of his illness was his inability to sleep. Thus we may question whether the temptation would not have been too strong even for his waking ego and would have caused him to yield consciously to masturbation. In any event, he saved himself from this fate by going back to sleep again and finding himself numerous times the victim of nocturnal emissions!

Let us try to sharpen our metapsychological insight into this final phase of Schreber's prepsychotic development. This prepsychotic phase is marked by the tendency toward regression. A return to infantile ego states takes place; or, to say it more metapsychologically, increasingly the libido cathects narcissistic positions. On this regressive level, the libido to a large extent is withdrawn from the object world. This regressive trend does not lead to a strengthening of the ego at the cost of the object world, but the process points to a return to the undifferentiated state. The loss of cathexis of the ego goes hand in hand with the loss of cathexis of the representations of the object world. The ego, in its struggle for self-preservation, clings increasingly to those objects that fulfill its narcissistic ideal. In order to clarify what this narcissistic ideal is, let us repeat: the danger is the occurrence of genital excitement. The ego attempts to master this excitement by relinquishing the masculine function, and projects the latter onto Flechsig. Through this projection, Flechsig becomes to an even greater degree Schreber's ideal of masculinity. We realize that this narcissistic ideal—Flechsig—represents Schreber's own masculinity which he has relinquished. Yet this idealization causes Flechsig to excel even more in those qualities which arouse Schreber's femininity. Therefore the defensive measures taken by his ego to fight the excitement are in danger of being undone again.

At this point we may advance a hypothesis as to why Schreber's excitement leads to an orgastic discharge. The danger, as I have just described, forces the ego to still more regressive mechanisms, so that the ego finally makes use of primary identifications as the form of its object relationships. Schreber's strong sexual feelings for Flechsig can now be expressed through this primary identification, for at this level the attachment to another object and the identification with that object are one. In this way the attraction to Flechsig leads to a merging of Schreber's ego with the idealized object (Flechsig)—a process culminating in Schreber's orgastic feelings.

It becomes clear what has happened. For defensive reasons, Schreber is engaged in the admiration of Flechsig's masculinity, focusing upon Flechsig's penis instead of upon his own. This defensive projection is eradicated by his primary identification with the admired object. Thus the two valencies of his bisexuality are united, and this union is expressed in orgasm. We have already stressed the fact that here orgasm and castration are bound together. Thus we see that the merging comprises the ego and the representation of the object, as well as the urge toward femininity. In order for the ego to cope with the danger, a withdrawal of cathexis of all the components involved must take place; i.e., that particular part of the ego, the object representation, and also the urge toward femininity, all lose their cathexis. Once this withdrawal of energy has taken place, the psychotic attempt at restitution takes over. It is clear that these three components—ego, object representation, and feminine urge—comprise only a part of the personality. The rest is not involved in the psychotic process, and at times when this particular conflict is not aroused, this remnant of the old personality can be very prominent.

We are now able to understand Schreber's "wonderful building-up of the hereafter" much better. In the hereafter he will be able to have intercourse as a woman, and thus he clings to the same desire as it was already revealed some time after his appointment as *Senatspräsident*. Yet the fulfillment of his desire underwent certain changes, which we are now able to explain through our comparison.

Schreber is not striving toward fulfillment during his lifetime, but postpones this until after death. Then no living person can exert an influence upon him any longer. Therefore he will be safe.

We also gain insight into how Schreber thinks he will be able to deal in the hereafter with the danger revolving around an orgasm. There will be continuation of life after death, and the first period of this continuation will contain his castration during the process of purification. Once this act is performed, he will not have to be bothered by reactions of his penis and he may indulge in a continuous masturbation fantasy. The satisfaction will lie in the enjoyment of beholding God, which we have translated as meaning that he will enjoy looking at his own projected masculinity. Schreber's remark that masculine bliss is of a higher order than feminine bliss points out clearly how much he would have preferred to have an orgasm of his penis while fantasying that he was a woman submitting to intercourse. Yet this would have meant destruction (castration). At this point we have to stress that the danger for Schreber did not lie in the mere wish to be a woman but was contained in the accompanying reaction of his penis. As soon as he could exclude penis orgasm, as in the hereafter, he could yield completely to the wish to be a woman.

Schreber's plan of the hereafter begins with his own castration. Yet after castration has taken place, the plan contains full provision for it to be undone again. The eternal round, with the support of Schreber's voyeurism, provides that everything which is lost will return.

As a side issue, we understand also why Schreber could not believe in Christ's resurrection. To his thinking, this dogma symbolized the resurrection of his penis. The acceptance of this dogma would have brought the return of the danger.

Indeed, Schreber possessed a "wonderful building-up of the hereafter." The only weakness lay in the fact that he remained silent about the way he would exclude the influence of his fellow men, of whom Flechsig was the chief representative.

So far we have interpreted exclusively the meaning of Schreber's delusions. Delusions are based upon absolute narcissism. Although they appear to occupy themselves with the outer world, it is easy to see that the outer world is the product of "narcissistic projection." The delusional outer world is nothing else than an externalized part of the id (or less frequently of the ego or superego). I shall not further expand on this idea, but, in order to furnish some clarification, cite two forms of projection. We have discussed how during the last part of Schreber's prepsychotic phase Flechsig, through projection, became Schreber's "narcissistic ideal object." This form of projection was a defense of a nonpsychotic nature. It had the task of focusing upon Flechsig's masculinity in order to keep Schreber's own masculinity—in a stricter sense, his genital excitement—under control.

The psychotic projection through which Schreber projected his masculinity onto the back realms of God has broken away from reality, whereas the nonpsychotic projection has not. In the psychotic projection, the masculinity within the boundaries of the psychotic part of the personality no longer exists; through projection, it has become outer world. These remarks conclude the discussion of the delusions of Schreber's first chapter, "God and Immortality," and we can now begin to study another aspect of the hereafter.

B. The Nonpsychotic Meaning of the Content
of the Delusion and Its Infantile Origin

In the preceding part we have followed the desire to be a woman submitting to intercourse from the prepsychotic state through the psychosis proper. Thus we see demonstrated again the true function of the delusion. Namely, a delusion is the result of the attempt at restitution to solve a conflict by unrealistic means, when the ego has previously been unable to cope with this conflict in a more realistic way. Yet the fact that this trend toward femininity was revealed during the prepsychotic state does not mean that this instinctual urge was formed at precisely that time. We understand very well that although the personality as a whole—i.e., not limited solely to the ego—has changed considerably, nevertheless whatever is present in the mind at that stage has strong roots in the preceding development from early childhood on. Notwithstanding the fact that the psychotic mechanisms deviate completely from the mechanisms which are under the guidance of reality thinking, we may conclude that through this chain of events the content of the psychotic symptoms may reflect not only prepsychotic but also infantile material.

We should keep well in mind the necessity for the content of the delusion to fulfill the need for expressing the state of absolute narcissism inherent in the psychosis. We may even say that this is the only provision which has to be fulfilled. Yet the fulfillment of this essential task does not preclude the possibility that the same content may be simultaneously the result of nonpsychotic or even neurotic mechanisms. Under certain circumstances, the occurrence side by side of two completely different groups of mechanisms, resulting in one and the same content, takes place, to my knowledge, in those cases in which a strong paranoialike feature appears in the foreground. Schreber certainly betrays such features, for does he not want to prove to mankind, by the publication of his autobiography, the truth of his convictions? Here we are appropriately reminded that Freud in 1922 (p. 221) pointed to the overlapping of various layers in paranoia.[8] It is the triumph of what I like to call an economic principle when a single content can serve simultaneously the demands of both psychotic and nonpsychotic mechanisms.

A good starting point for our purpose is the process of purification and its related acquisition of the "ground-language." The process of purification was the essential step toward the state of bliss in the hereafter and enabled Schreber to get rid of his genital sexuality; the latter had been the cause of severe castration anxiety ever since the beginning of his illness. During the process of purification, the souls learned the "ground-language," which was spoken by God. We know from the footnote which Schreber appended to the ex-

[8] In a subsequent publication I shall discuss the peculiar fact that Schreber's schizophrenia, during the period of 1900–1903, preceding publication of his autobiography, acquired increasingly a paranoialike feature.

pression "forecourts of heaven" that the "ground-language" was revealed to him by the voices. He denied any knowledge of this language or insight into its origin. The words were not his own invention; he had never heard them used by other people, and they were partially of a scientific nature, in particular of a medical nature.

In general, the "ground-language," as we have already pointed out, is a somewhat old-fashioned but nevertheless powerful German, which is especially characterized by its great wealth of euphemisms. Indeed, such expressions as "in consideration of the one who is and will be," "Eternal Majesty yours faithfully obedient," "forecourts of heaven," etc., sound "somewhat old-fashioned" also to us. We may remark that these expressions sound so exaggerated as to border on the ridiculous in their pomposity. Yet souls who were in training to become part of the forecourts of heaven had to learn the language appropriate to the deity, and as such these rather strange expressions have at least a very clear meaning. To bestow upon God the appellation "in consideration of the one who is and will be" emphasizes very well the importance of God's eternal existence. When we discussed the delusional meaning of the purification, we concluded that the language itself was the product of the purification; also that the use of certain words with their meaning reversed expressed the primary aim of the process of purification, namely, to transform Schreber into a woman.

These findings should assist in our further exploration. God used this language; and Schreber, by becoming purified, would be able to acquire this language too. Of course, from early childhood on, Schreber had formed a certain idea of God. In this connection we are reminded of Freud's penetrating analysis through which he revealed the relationship between Schreber's god and his own father. Freud (1911) explained very convincingly that Schreber's critical attitude toward his father had carried over to God. Our next conclusion is now quickly drawn: *the "ground-language" reflects the language used by Schreber's father.*

As we have heard, Schreber does not know anything about such a relationship. Nevertheless, it remains conspicuous that the words of the "ground-language" are partly of a scientific and more especially of a medical nature; this latter fact is important, for Schreber's father was a physician. From Freud's article, we learn that the father was a man who tried to raise the standards of health and whose name is kept alive by the numerous Schreber associations and the wide circulation of his *Ärztliche Zimmergymnastik* (*Medical Indoor Gymnastics*). It would be appropriate for such a man to speak in the manner portrayed by the "ground-language." He would have used "old-fashioned," long-winded expressions which impressed one by their pomposity. At certain times he would have put *force* into his words through the use of certain powerful terms and would have described a number of situations in a *"euphemistic"* way.

Having gone so far, we feel compelled to examine ideas such as "devils" and "purification." As a result, our attention is automatically drawn to the peculiarity that the souls during their purification are called in the "ground-language" *"devils."* What else can we conclude than that Schreber's father many times called his son a "devil" when he was dissatisfied with his son's behavior? For we know that the father did not shrink from the use of powerful words heightened by exaggeration.

If we can relate the word "devil" to Schreber's childhood, we may do so even more with the word *"purification,"* which the voices called a *"test."* According to the content of the delusion, during the process of purification man will be transformed into woman. Unless we resort to the assumption that masculinity is simply dirty, we should like to know why this religious procedure is called purification. At this point we are reminded of the repugnant odor and peculiar coloring of certain devils when they were placed in Schreber's environment. These devils were souls in the process of being purified, which is synonymous with being "tested." This examination lasted for the entire extent of the purification. Therefore the souls were being "tested" all the time. The repugnant odor and peculiar reddish coloring certainly point to a heightened anal activity.[9] Thus we have added to the process of transformation into a woman the fact that during the purifying process, anal symptoms also became strongly noticeable.[10]

Indeed, the term "purification" fits very well the anal training of the child. Yet we have already discovered that the phallic phase also is included, for during the purification process man will be transformed into woman. Thus the process of purification covers a prominent part of Schreber's childhood development. The attitudes which the child formed during the anal period under the influence of his father's upbringing must have laid the foundation for his behavior during the phallic phase.

Why was this continual testing necessary? The answer no longer causes us many difficulties. It becomes increasingly clear that the delusional process of purification reflects a childhood period when thoughts of loss of masculinity haunted this little boy, and anal difficulties were many. Now we understand why the testing played such an important role. Schreber's father tried to keep the little boy's behavior under constant scrutiny, whether he was abusing his penis or was impure in an anal sense. This period was called purification. No doubt the little Schreber learned at that time to speak the "ground-

[9] Niederland (1951) has already pointed out that the odor and color should be conceived of as having an anal meaning.

[10] It may appear that in my interpretation I have attached too much significance to this hint at an anal meaning as it is contained in the repugnant odor and peculiar coloring of the devils. I may add that in the later course of Schreber's psychosis the anal trends became increasingly clear. For instance, Dr. Weber stated that Schreber soiled himself. Schreber on various occasions mentioned his anal symptoms; for instance, in the part which is quoted by Freud (1911, p. 26). I will, of course, discuss this material extensively in later publications.

language": he learned to obey the "somewhat old-fashioned" but "powerful" German which was characterized by its great wealth of euphemisms. This was the language spoken by his father. The vigor and accompanying characteristics of the language forced the little boy into a state of extreme anxiety so that he thought he would lose his penis, and at the same time there was an increase of anal activity. From the fact that God looked at his own creations, we may deduce that the little boy had the feeling that his father's eye was continually upon him. This watching was a part of the testing.

The euphemisms are the only detail of the "ground-language" which we have not yet dealt with properly. Schreber remarked that souls that had not yet gone through the process of purification were not given the name "untested souls," as one might expect, but, in accordance with the tendency toward euphemisms, exactly the reverse, "tested souls." This remark thus stresses that the reversal of meaning of the words was called "euphemism" by Schreber. Other examples are "reward" for "punishment"; "poison" for "food"; "juice" for "poison"; and "unsacred" for "sacred."

This reversal of the meaning of words not only reflects the transformation of man into woman. We know that when children play with words, reversing their meaning, or when they become a little bit older and read words backward, this play has practically always an anal connotation: the back side becomes the front side, and playing with feces is displaced onto words.

Yet the question remains: why are these words whose meanings have been changed into the reverse, examples of "euphemisms"? I would say that a euphemism protrays something in too favorable a light, that it glosses over its faults. Therefore, in a euphemism a denial-like quality becomes apparent.

For the sake of better understanding of this denial-like quality, let us concentrate upon Schreber's statement that punishment in the hereafter does not exist. The facts do not prove the validity of this statement, for submitting to the process of purification was regarded by the souls as a disagreeable task which they were forced to perform. They had to pass through various interim stages in which they were called devils. Judas Iscariot, for example, because of his betrayal of Jesus Christ, had been a "ground devil" (p. 14). Moreover, Schreber himself admitted that to apply the name of punishment in these instances was to a certain extent correct. Thus the problem is: why did Schreber have to negate the existence of punishment in the hereafter? We are already acquainted with Schreber's defense that if we want to call the treatment to which the devils were submitted a form of punishment, we should not forget that this punishment was not inflicted for the sake of punishment but served only as a preparatory stage to the attainment of a state of bliss. *Thus the punishment was inflicted for the devil's own good.*

Let us turn now to the euphemism that *punishment is called a "reward."* This euphemism expresses precisely what we have just said about the absence of punishment in the hereafter. We may follow with the example of the *"tested souls."* To submit someone relentlessly to testing, thus showing this person one's great distrust, and then still calling the person tested, is certainly a euphemism![11]

We now know enough to supplement our interpretation of the meaning of the process of purification. We have a mental picture of a father who does not punish his son for the sake of punishment, but for the child's own good —a father who wants to drive the "devil" out of his son, who wants to make his son pure so that he will not masturbate again and will not spread "repugnant odors" or, even worse, soil himself, as we may deduce from the description of a peculiar reddish coloring. Such a father deserves the name of hypocrite. Under cover of having his son's interests at heart, he submits him to a treatment of relentless testing and tongue-lashing, which Schreber so appropriately called the "ground-language." I think we are not far wrong in calling this upbringing sadistic. At least we find confirmation of this opinion if we keep in mind that this punishment served only as a preparatory stage to the attainment of a state of bliss. This blissful state is of a feminine nature and consists of uninterrupted enjoyment in beholding God. From this delusional content, we are able to deduce the way in which Schreber reacted to his father's treatment. *A feminine masochistic attitude was the result: Schreber surrendered his own masculinity and admired his father's masculinity instead.* In this way a scoptophilic tendency came to the fore. We shall discuss this important point later. The names used by his father to convey meanings that were practically the opposite of what his treatment really amounted to, Schreber in a still kindly way called "euphemisms." From the simple fact that Schreber tried to keep all harshness out of the names, we may deduce that he wanted to ward off to the utmost his criticism of his father. It is in the disparity between his father's words and his father's actions that I think we should conceive of the expression "euphemisms" as used by Schreber.

Still another subject awaits us. Who are the devils? We have already touched upon this subject in passing. Schreber has pictured these devils as creatures of a rather tame nature who bear no relation to the evil spirit which the Devil is usually portrayed as being. We have just concluded that Schreber tried to deny that the devils were punished mercilessly. Even Judas Iscariot, for his betrayal of Christ, is punished by becoming a ground devil for only a certain period of time; this latter concept is, in Schreber's mind, still of a very innocent nature. Notwithstanding Schreber's attempts to picture these devils as not being devilish at all, we still must conclude that they are held in great disfavor because God did not like their features.

We have even gone much further in our interpretation and deduced from the material concerning the devils far-reaching conclusions about Schreber himself. That is, we have taken it for granted that the devils represented

---

[11] The euphemisms "poison" for "food," "juice" for "poison," "unsacred" for "sacred" are connected with Schreber's relationship to Flechsig. Since the latter is not mentioned in the first chapter, we do not want to complicate things and will discuss the meaning of these words alongside of the material in *Denkwürdigkeiten*, Chapter V, pp. 58 ff.

various aspects of Schreber himself. We have even conjectured that his father, when he caught Schreber in one of his sinful acts, called him a devil and wanted to stamp the devil out of him. In other words, we have interpreted the devils as projections of certain features of Schreber's own self. Their core is the infantile part with the masturbatory and anal tendencies. The warding off of these tendencies under the influence of his father's forceful actions presumably led Schreber to a feminine masochistic attitude toward his father.

The way in which Schreber treats the subject of devils is very interesting. According to our understanding, the devils are projections of Schreber's own dangerous unconscious instincts. Once they are projected, Schreber tries to deny their vicious character by saying they are already very "God-fearing."

In the "ground-language" the word "ground" denotes "cause." "Ground-language" is a very appropriate expression, for it embraces a large part of Schreber's childhood neurosis.

Schreber, in the hereafter, will take over his father's language, but not without changing it. For instance, in addition to the exaggerations, there are many high-sounding words, about which Schreber explicitly remarked that he had never heard them before and knew them only through the voices. The fact that they were new to him could be used in support of his denial of the connection they had with the language of his father. On the other hand, they were words which his father had certainly never used and were intentionally made up to show his father's pomposity. Similarly, the entire language still bears in one aspect the imprint of Schreber's fear and awe of his father; and, on the other hand, through the tremendous exaggerations, Schreber expresses his derision. Schreber has applied what Freud called the *"Retourkutsche"*; he bounces back what his father has thrown at him. If his father preaches that the little Schreber should be thankful for the tongue-lashings, his son shows his derisive criticism by turning a number of words around: for instance, "reward" means "punishment." This conclusion is the result of our analysis; otherwise one would not be able to make head or tail out of it. In this way Schreber made his aggression unrecognizable.

It is now time to discuss Schreber's feminine-masochistic attitude, which we have mentioned only in passing. His father's testing, we concluded, started in the anal phase and extended through the phallic phase which followed. We may even assume that his father would have continued keeping an eye on his son's behavior until he (the father) died.

We conclude that Schreber's father was far from being successful. Instead of the testing having a controlling effect, it excited the boy considerably. In stressing this last statement, we are reminded of the following.

On very rare occasions, although still in harmony with the "world order," God could "take a nerve attachment" to a *living* man of exceptional talent in order to inspire that man with fertile thoughts about the hereafter. There was danger involved in such a development, for if the nerves of that living man in communication with God became inordinately excited, they would exert such a strong attraction upon the nerves of God that the latter nerves could no longer free themselves, and God's own existence would then be threatened. Therefore such a situation was not permitted to occur very often.

This quotation makes it completely clear that Schreber as a child was very much excited sexually by his father. At first sight, it seems strange that this could happen in accordance with the "world order." Thus we conclude that for the child the "world order" was the daily rule laid down by his father, and, what is more important, that his father's routine excited the boy intensely. The quotation also reveals that if this excitement became a regular occurrence, the point of an emergency would be reached. God's existence would then be threatened, for he would not be able to liberate himself.

Considering Schreber's way of reacting, we must admit that if the father had discovered his son's genital excitement, the end of the "world order" would have occurred. As for the rest, we may assume that it had to do with a projection, for the boy must have feared becoming completely spellbound by his father and must have felt his own existence threatened. Only in the course of later events does Schreber provide us with more material about this extraordinary situation of God being endangered.

We should like to know much more about Schreber's excitement under the influence of his relationship with his father. Was Schreber's penis aroused by this relationship, and did this relationship have any ties with his positive oedipus complex, provided he had such a complex?

In the delusional content, Schreber's excitement would endanger the existence of God; we have already concluded, therefore, that even in his psychotic state there was at least the possibility that he would become genitally aroused. Thus the chances are pretty good that in his childhood Schreber's genitals were aroused.

Whether there was any connection between Schreber's excitement and his positive oedipus complex, is a difficult question to answer. His excitement impresses us as being simply the result of the peculiarly sadistic way in which his father treated him.

So far we have not detected any influence of Schreber's mother upon him. At this point we are reminded of the feminine front realms of God. If the back realms represent the picture of Schreber's father in childhood, then the front realms undoubtedly stand for his mother. God floating above the front realms was symbolic of intercourse. With the two realms of God united in intercourse, it is suddenly revealed to us that Schreber is speaking of the primal scene. The result of his observations must have lead to an identification with his mother. We remember that masculine bliss was of a higher order than feminine bliss—a statement which, in my opinion, points to the existence of at least a wish on Schreber's part to identify with his father. Yet clearly his father's upbringing, through the castration threat, made such an outcome impossible.

Thus it gradually becomes clear that a positive oedipus complex did exist. We may add that Schreber became psychotic only relatively late in life. Before, he had been able to function very well. Personally, I doubt whether such functioning would have been possible without the foundation of a positive oedipus complex. We may say that the already existing femininity influenced the formation of his oedipus complex, whereupon, as a result of the castration threats, the final result, after passing through the oedipal phase, was an increase in femininity.

Such an increase in femininity does not necessarily have to lead to a homosexual perversion; in certain cases even potency, as far as an erection is concerned, does not have to be affected. I know of cases where potency is maintained through the use of the identification with the female partner as a defense. The voyeurism of these patients, as they look through the eyes of the woman at their own masculinity, affords them a certain enjoyment and defends them against the possibility of the erection disappearing under the influence of the castration danger. Instead of being on the losing end, they are on the receiving end because of the feminine identification, for then they have gotten their penis back. We have already had the opportunity to notice in Schreber certain features which bring within the realm of possibility such a solution during Schreber's more normal days.

We return now to Schreber's childhood. Using the eternal round as an example, the acceptance of the feminine role enabled Schreber to have the fantasy that he would produce children in the same way as his mother had done. As we have seen in our discussion of the delusion, these children would serve mainly the purpose of undoing an eventual castration. We may even conclude from Schreber's identification with the Virgin Mary (something similar to the Immaculate Conception had also taken place in Schreber's body) that he also wanted to deny the sexual relationship between his father and his mother.

We will do well not to confuse the ramifications of Schreber's infantile oedipal situation with the delusion portraying the "wonderful building-up of the hereafter." In Schreber's childhood, his femininity in its final form arose as the result of passing through the oedipus complex. Schreber's delusion about the hereafter does not have the oedipus complex as its base. There is only the contact between his femininity and his projected masculinity, and phallic and even anal sexuality are abolished. Yet this was possible only in the hereafter.

Thus the overwhelming danger of the prepsychotic phase already has an example in childhood. But whereas in childhood a solution was found within the frame of the reality principle, such a solution was not possible once the destructive process of the psychosis came into full swing.

In the beginning of my interpretation of this chapter, I remarked that Schreber had reserved a part of himself that was never satisfied during his lifetime, to be compensated in the hereafter. We now know that Schreber suffered from his relationship with his father, and we can follow his compensatory trends all through his delusion of the hereafter.

In the hereafter there will not be, in contradistinction to the overpowering father of Schreber's childhood, an all-knowing God who is ever-present. God does not look into the hearts of human beings. After all the testing that Schreber's father has done in the past, Schreber's future father, of whom Schreber subsequently will become a part, will have given up this task.

We have deduced that in Schreber's childhood, his father's eye rested upon him continually. From this we may assume that the self-observing function of Schreber's superego was well developed. The following quotation illustrates this point admirably: "Before his illness *Senatspräsident* Schreber had been a man of strict morals: 'Few people,' he declares, and I see no reason to doubt his assertion, 'can have been brought up upon such strict moral principles as I was, and few people, all through their lives, can have exercised (especially in sexual matters) a self-restraint conforming so closely to those principles as I may say of myself that I have done' (p. 281)" (Freud, 1911, p. 31). Before his illness "he had been inclined to sexual asceticism and had been a doubter in regard to God" (p. 29) (Freud, 1911, p. 32). Not only did Schreber's God of the hereafter still carry the traces of Schreber's religious unbelief as a protest against his father, but in his psychosis he had also freed himself to a certain extent from the shackles of his confining superego. We agree fully that Schreber had a right to get rid of the torturing father and his too restrictive superego.

In contrast to the forbidden masturbation, in the hereafter Schreber will indulge in an uninterrupted masturbation, although we must admit that its orgasm will be considerably reduced, so much so, that genitality will be abolished. Schreber will be able to yield to an aggressive criticism of his father, although here, too, this trend will have to be restricted, for it has had to be carefully hidden. Thus, gradually a picture developed in which the self-promised freedom in the hereafter became a very vulnerable matter. Eternity, together with various other defenses, was used as a defense against the danger of castration; denial played a major supportive role in this defensive struggle, although the devils, to be sure, were not kept so completely under control as would be desirable for the restful peace of the hereafter.

Next, we remember that God's existence could be threatened under special conditions. Although we do not know the meaning of this particular delusion, it is a further proof of the vulnerability of the structure of the hereafter, in which Schreber has promised himself so much compensation for all his suffering. . . .

16 / The Mother-Conflict in Schreber's Psychosis[1]

Robert B. White

It is my basic hypothesis that primitive, oral, destructive-dependent impulses towards a mother-figure were a crucial component of Schreber's psychotic conflict. The symbolic representation of that mother-figure and of the oral impulses directed towards her are, I believe, the most prominent and consistent themes in the *Memoirs*. The devastating effect of these oral impulses is demonstrated by Schreber's delusional conviction that first his wife, then Flechsig, and eventually all humanity had died, and that God himself was in grave danger of extinction. That Schreber's pregenital, dependent, voracious impulses were the cause of this destruction, and that the wife, Flechsig, and God were to a large degree representations of the mother towards whom these impulses were directed, can, I believe, be demonstrated in the *Memoirs*.

.   .   .

In June of 1893, the Minister of Justice personally informed Schreber of his "impending appointment as *Senatspräsident* to the Superior Court in Dresden," the Supreme Court of Saxony to which only the Imperial German High Court in Leipzig was superior. Niederland (6) states that promotion to this court meant a "practically irreversible life status" for Schreber, and "refusal [of the appointment] would have been something like a crime . . . , since such promotions were made by the King . . . and could not be refused. Illness, then, was the only way out, and with a lifelong position of this kind as a permanent threat before the patient, it could not be of short duration."

Schreber himself emphasizes that his second illness was caused by the heavy burden of work of his new post. Between his appointment in June and his assuming office on 1 October, 1893, he dreamed several times of a recurrence of his nervous illness. In addition, shortly after awaking one morning, he had the strange thought that it must really be pleasant to be a woman succumbing to intercourse. Schreber indignantly rejected this idea which seemed so foreign to his whole nature, and he later decided that the experience was a result of malicious, external influences. It seems clear that Schreber's defences were failing before he assumed his new office. Premonitory dreams and regressive fantasies had begun to occur. As later discussion will support, in

[1] Excerpts reprinted from the *International Journal of Psycho-Analysis*, Vol. 42 (1961), Pts. 1–2, with the author's permission.

addition to its oedipal significance, Schreber's homosexual fantasy of being a woman also expressed an intense longing to give up the status of an adult man and, by identification with the pregenital mother, to regress to an archaic, undifferentiated, oral-dependent fusion with her.

. . .

If, as Ferenczi (3) suggested, adult sexual intimacy is at one level a symbolic return to the womb, that is, a symbolic merging again with the mother, it is all the more understandable that Schreber's latent, primitive longing for such a total fusion with the mother might have become pathogenically intense at the time of his marriage. In ego-psychological terms, Erikson (1) deals with this issue in his description of the crisis of intimacy versus isolation when he states: "Body and ego must now be masters of the organ modes and of the nuclear conflicts, in order to be able to face the fear of ego loss in situations which call for self-abandon: in orgasms and sexual unions, in close friendships and in physical combat, in experiences of inspiration by teachers and of intuition from the recesses of the self. The avoidance of such experiences because of a fear of ego loss may lead to a deep sense of isolation and consequent self-absorption." Loewald (4) has also discussed these questions, suggesting that the fear of loss of ego through regression to the "primary narcissistic identity with the mother" is one of man's deepest dreads— the dread of the "engulfing, overpowering womb." Federn (2) has, of course, also dealt extensively with the sense of loss of the ego, but not in terms directly relevant here.

. . .

Schreber's image of his mother was fused with that of the father. The mother was, to a great extent, an agent of the father who clearly was the higher power behind her. She probably was as thoroughly dominated by the father as were the frightened nannies of Leipzig. The father was, after all, one of the leading authorities on child rearing in *all* Germany as well as a person of awesome personal characteristics.

Not only was the father a trespasser on the maternal realms, he was an ambivalent trespasser deeply divided in his intent. On the one hand, he intruded into those very private matters between mother and baby out of the most worthy medical motive and out of the most understandable paternal hope—to ensure that his son developed into a strong, morally sound, healthy man, free of weak, childish, or effeminate traits. On the other hand, his intrusion into the mother's role was such a fanatical and vengeful one that it arouses suspicions that other motives were at work—suspicions that the intrusion was both a defence against the father's own intense, possessive, needful (homosexual, if you like) longings, and an expression of his intense envy and jealousy of the nursing baby. The cruel teasing of the child with the mother's pear was quite probably a vengeful withholding from the child of that which the father himself secretly wanted and envied. What more fitting revenge can a son later inflict upon such a father than to become the very kind of person the father most feared that he himself was and that the son would be? In turning his back upon the crowning achievement of a brilliant career and regressing to the primitive level of his psychosis, Schreber did exactly that. He thus symbolically repossessed the mother, mocked and defied the father, and punished himself for doing both.

.   .   .

For a time after Schreber believed his wife was dead, he considered Flechsig the only person whom he "knew definitely to be among the living" (5, p. 70)—the sole object of his hopes, needs, and impulses. Then, like Schreber's wife, Flechsig deserted him for a vacation. In Schreber's delusions Flechsig met a violent and deserved death on this holiday trip which took place in March, just a month after the wife's "fatal" holiday. Schreber "had visions [that] . . . Flechsig had shot himself." These visions were, he noted, "revelations of divine opinion on what *ought* to have happened to Professor Flechsig" (p. 91). The lost Flechsig was then immediately regained by primitive, oral incorporation.

After Flechsig "shot himself," Schreber commented, "about that time I had Professor Flechsig's soul and most probably his *whole* soul temporarily in my body. It was a fairly bulky ball . . . , which had been thrown into my belly by way of a miracle, presumably to perish there. In view of its size it would . . . have been impossible to retain this soul in my belly, to digest it so to speak; indeed when it attempted to free itself I let it go voluntarily, being moved by a kind of sympathy, and so it escaped through my mouth into the open again. I have . . . in quite a number of other instances . . . received souls or parts of souls in my mouth, of which I particularly remember distinctly the foul taste and smell which such *impure* souls cause in the body of the person through whose mouth they have entered."

.   .   .

Schreber's wife was orally incorporated with fatal consequences when she deserted him for her holiday of which she was in urgent need, apparently having been as depleted as the anterior realms of God later became. Finally, then, it is God Himself who is in danger of annihilation by Schreber's oral impulses—impulses which are projected as the irresistible need of God's nerves to flow into Schreber's body. Nearly irrefutable evidence that Schreber projects onto God his destructively needful, pregenital, oral impulses towards a mother-figure is present in his reference to Goethe's poem, "The Fisherman," of which he quotes only one line. Schreber could hardly have picked a more perfect artistic statement than this poem to express his own primitive wishes to merge with a mother, to possess her exclusively, to return to the healing peace of her inside, to be made *sound* again by the nurture he receives from her, to rip ruthlessly from her belly competitors for that nurture. It also expresses his fear of again being engulfed by the mother—a danger which stemmed largely from the intensity of his own needfulness for her. . . .

.   .   .

SUMMARY AND CONCLUSIONS

On theoretical grounds, it is reasonable to assume that primitive, oral, destructive-dependent impulses towards a mother-figure were important in the dynamics of Schreber's psychosis. Reanalysis of the *Memoirs* shows that disguised and symbolic representations of the mother and of such impulses towards her were, in fact, prominent in the case. The new historical data on Schreber's breakdowns and family also support this assumption. The basic defence which Schreber used against such impulses was that of projection— accusing God of needful, greedy, potentially destructive, oral longings for Schreber when in fact it was Schreber's jealous, possessive, infantile longing for God which was symbolically represented as "nerve-contact," which motivated "soul murder," and which threatened to destroy the entire world and even God Himself. Schreber's delusion of being unmanned was at one level an expression of the wish to regain that most primitive and least differentiated relation of the child to the mother which is enjoyed by the foetus. By being unmanned in the peculiar manner of his delusions, Schreber was simultaneously the foetus and the mother who carries the foetus.

The merged mother and father images in the God of Schreber's delusions, a God composed of maternal anterior realms and paternal posterior realms, quite likely reflected the intrusive way in which the father invaded the mother's role and function in Schreber's early infancy. The further division of these paternal posterior realms into a superior god of Goodness, Ormuzd, and an inferior god of Evil, Ahriman, was probably based on Schreber's infantile image of his pathologically ambivalent father.

17 / The Schreber Case Reconsidered in the Light of Psycho-Social Concepts[1]

Robert B. White

My reconsideration of the case will be made in terms of Erikson's concepts of psycho-social stages of personality development. Space does not allow an extensive effort to relate this view of the case to the other new concepts of ego-psychology or to the basic concepts of libido theory, particularly the concept of psychosexual stages of development; I reconsider the case, therefore, in terms of only one of the several sets of new concepts that have been placed at our disposal in recent years, and I largely omit consideration of libido theory. Let me emphasize a point that has not been sufficiently noted by many authors who have restudied the Schreber case, a point especially ignored by Macalpine and Hunter (1955); a study of any case from any one point of view, libido-concepts, ego-concepts, or psycho-social concepts, must be incomplete. Freud's (1911) formulations were made in terms of libido theory and of the Oedipus complex. These were the concepts, and the only ones, then available. They are obviously incomplete in the light of our present knowledge. But a study of the case from any one of our more modern points of view only would be equally incomplete.

. . .

Erikson's theory of psycho-social development, an epigenetic theory, is especially noteworthy because it is the only systematic psycho-analytic conceptualization of the stages of development of personality beyond adolescence. Concepts of personality development that emphasize the importance of the events of adult years as well as those of childhood and adolescence are especially helpful in understanding the onset of Schreber's breakdowns, something otherwise difficult to explain, as Freud himself noted.

According to Erikson, the human develops at the embryological level according to a pre-determined ground plan during the pre-natal period, and his development continues in an equally orderly fashion at the social, interpersonal level from birth onward to senescence. He believes that the development of the child's personality "obeys and on the whole can be trusted to obey inner laws of development, namely those laws which in the [the] pre-natal period had formed one organ after another and which [in the post-

[1] Excerpts reprinted from the *International Journal of Psycho-Analysis*, Vol. 44, (1963), Pt. 2, with the author's permission.

natal period] create a succession of potentialities for significant interaction with [others] around him" (Erikson, 1950, p. 63).

He proposes eight stages in the development of personality each of which arises in a predetermined sequence and at a phase-specific point of the human life cycle. Here is a chart [Editor's note: chart is omitted; it can be found in Dr. White's original paper.] of the psycho-social stages of development in Schreber's life compiled from data now available from the work of Baumeyer (1956), Macalpine and Hunter (1955, 1956), Niederland (1951, 1959a-b, 1960), and myself.

As the foregoing shows, each psycho-social stage of development is designated by a pair of nouns of more or less opposite meanings—trust versus mistrust, autonomy versus shame and doubt, and so on. Each of these eight stages culminates in a developmental crisis that results from a "decisive encounter" (Erikson, 1959, p. 53) between the person and his environment. As new capacities and a new perspective on life evolve at each new stage the person must have yet another decisive encounter with his environment and its particular ideas of the values and behavior that are desirable in a person of his age if he is to continue to develop into the kind of person the society needs. The outcome of this encounter determines the basic position the person will take somewhere between the polar extremes for that stage. For example, take the stage of trust versus mistrust. Each infant, after the fundamental experience of being cared for by the mother, prepares to leave this stage of maximum dependency. If the baby has found the mother to be trustworthy, a maternal attribute that depends not only on how much the mother feels she can trust herself but also on how much she feels she can trust her spouse, her family, and her immediate community, then the child acquires a basically trusting attitude towards himself, other people, and later towards life and the hereafter. But no child finds it possible to trust completely. All his needs, some of which are innately insatiable, cannot be met. Every child, therefore, suffers some sense of disappointment, hurt, betrayal, and loss of the blissful unity he once had, or fantasied having, with the mother. From this inevitable trauma and from the host of others that might have been avoided if fate or parent had been kinder stems the reservoir of basic mistrust that is within all persons to varying degrees.

. . .

The father's medical writings on methods of childrearing give support to the assumption that Schreber's early childhood experiences quite likely created great difficulties for the resolution of his developmental crises of trust versus mistrust, autonomy versus shame and doubt, initiative versus guilt, and industry versus inferiority. We are indebted to Niederland (1951, 1959a-b, 1960) for much that we know of these publications of the father.

. . .

Of special relevance for Schreber's developmental stage of initiative versus guilt is his father's urgent plea for all parents to maintain an "incessant vigilance" against that "insidious plague of youth," masturbation, which, he states, ". . . makes the unfortunate [youngster] stupid and dumb, fed up with life, overly disposed to sickness, vulnerable to countless diseases of the lower abdomen and to diseases of the nervous system, and very soon makes them impotent as well as sterile" (Niederland, 1959b, p. 390). He was equally fierce in his comments to parents about pets for children, warning that the sadistic side of the child's nature would surely be unduly stimulated by the temptation to commit acts of cruelty to the animals.[2]

We know, of course, from data unearthed by Baumeyer that the elder Schreber himself suffered from an "obsessional neurosis with homicidal impulses" (1956, p. 62). We can reasonably assume that he also was in great conflict about his own impulses to masturbate—the fervor of his campaign to stamp out the practice betrays him badly.

The elder Schreber was apparently successful in his campaign to stamp out sensual and sadistic impulses in his son—at least for a time. Schreber states in his *Memoirs*, "few people have been brought up according to such strict moral principles as I, and have throughout life practised such moderation especially in matters of sex . . ." (Macalpine and Hunter, 1955, p. 208). In his psychotic regression, however, all that had been so ruthlessly stamped out in Schreber by parental force in his childhood returned with added fury. The *Memoirs* are replete with references to every form of pregenital and genital sexual acts and to the most primitive sorts of murderous rage. . . .

. . .

Although the good Doctor's system of childrearing seems exceedingly harsh to us, Erikson makes another point about such matters that is worth noting: ". . . a traditional system of child care can be said to be a factor making for trust, even where certain items of that tradition, taken singly, may seem irrational or unnecessarily cruel. Here much depends on whether such items are inflicted on the child by the parent in the firm traditional belief that this is the only way to do things or whether the parent misuses his administration of the baby and the child in order to work off anger, alleviate fear, or win an argument, with the child or with somebody else (mother-in-law, doctor, or priest)" (Erikson, 1959, p. 63).

Dr. Schreber's methods may have helped both to resolve his son's oedipal conflict and to arm him for the onslaught of instinctual tensions of adolescence and the crisis of identity versus identity diffusion. Concerning this crisis of identity versus identity diffusion in Schreber's life, we have few data. I can only conjecture that he weathered the storms of puberty reasonably well because of his intense identification with his compulsive father. This identifica-

---

[2] For these data about the senior Schreber's views on pets I am indebted to my colleague, Hendrik Lindt, for his excellent translation of a section of Dr. Schreber's book, *Das Buch der Erziehung an Leib und Seele* (1865). Dr. Norman Reider kindly gave me access to this volume from his personal library.

tion probably helped considerably in the management of the instinctual con-flicts of childhood and adolescence, but, as we noted earlier, it may well have made Schreber vulnerable to the adult problems of intimacy versus isolation. It was when he reached the crisis of intimacy versus isolation that Schreber's severe difficulties became manifest. The hypochondriasis that occurred at the time of his engagement to be married warned of the approach of the paranoid and hypochondriacal psychotic symptoms that overwhelmed him during his generativity crisis six years later after a defeat in politics and the first two stillborn children.

18 / Observations on Paranoia and their Relationship to the Schreber Case[1]

Arthur C. Carr

This paper includes a brief review and evaluation of the major criticisms of the traditional theory of paranoia, followed by some general observations on paranoia regarding such issues as the role of hostility, the essential nature of a delusion, the megalomaniac aspects implicit in all delusions, and rationalization as a defence. An attempt will be made to relate these observations, where pertinent, to the Schreber psychopathology.

Although Freud's (1911) interpretation of the Schreber autobiography has frequently been subject to attack and criticism, a survey of the vast literature accumulated on the Schreber case can only impress one with the wisdom and insight revealed by Freud in his original formulation. No alternative explanation or theory of paranoia has been proposed which has merited comparable consideration, respect, and acceptance.

Major criticism of the traditional theory of paranoia elucidated by Freud has been centered around the invariability of the role of unconscious homosexuality in the dynamics of the disorder, in terms of varying ways by which the proposition "I (a man) love him" presumably becomes transformed into a paranoid delusion. The striking contrast between Freud's formulation and the then current literature (e.g. Friedmann, 1908; Gierlich, 1908), however, would lead to the conclusion that Freud's primary contribution was perhaps not his elucidation of a relationship between homosexuality and paranoia, but rather was his demonstration of a way of thinking (the psychodynamic approach). Through application of the defense mechanism of *projection*, the psychopathology of paranoia was made meaningful in the context of motivational dynamics and understandable in the light of life's experience, in a way not previously accomplished.

The theory that paranoid delusions are always a defence against homosexuality has been challenged by evidence of two general types. First, many cases of paranoid symptomatology do not appear to reflect any homosexual problem. In one of the earlier reports challenging the Freudian theory, for example, Klein and Horwitz (1949) reviewed the case records of eighty patients selected from a group previously diagnosed as of paranoid state or

[1] Excerpts reprinted from the *International Journal of Psycho-Analysis*, Vol. 44 (1963), Pt. 2, with the author's permission.

schizophrenia, paranoid type. Only one-fifth of the group gave any expression of references assumed by the authors to have homosexual implications.

Further evidence in apparent opposition to the Freudian theory stems from case reports which demonstrate a co-existence of paranoid delusions and overt homosexuality, sometimes in patients who accept their homosexuality without apparent conflict.

. . .

Although the presence of both overt homosexuality and paranoia in the same patient would also seemingly challenge the adequacy of the Freudian theory, no contradiction exists when the basic distinction between conscious homosexuality and latent or unconscious homosexuality is kept in mind. Glick (1959) in a recent publication pertaining to homosexual panic, elaborates this distinction as follows: ". . . we must realize that manifest (conscious) and latent (unconscious) homosexuality are not one and the same thing; that they exist, speaking metaphorically and topographically, in different areas of the psychical system; that they pursue independent courses (the contents of the unconscious may always be considered to be unavailable to the ego and conscious mentation except through interpretation, and sometimes never available to consciousness under any circumstances), and that in a sense 'never the twain shall meet.' "

This distinction seems equally relevant for paranoia, where close inspection invariably reveals that the homosexual impulses being denied or reacted against are of quite a different kind from those which may reach overt expression. . . .

As a *theory*, Freud's formulation has stood up remarkably well, serving to organize, predict, and give meaning to behavior and facts not immediately apparent. For example, while Macalpine and Hunter insist that Freud's conclusion regarding homosexuality and castration threat in Schreber's dynamics was based on distortion and misinterpretation of "procreation fantasies," other evidence attests to its predictive value. Macalpine and Hunter (1955, p. 24) write as follows: "Freud's homosexual bias had led him to interpretation of castration anxieties in Schreber's illness, based more on theoretical preconceptions than on actual material. Indeed he appears to have misunderstood some of Schreber's fundamental delusions, such as being 'unmanned.' This was a fantasy of being transformed gradually over 'decades if not centuries' into a reproductive woman, carrying neither a castration threat nor passive homosexual wishes."

The recently presented hospital records (Baumeyer, 1956) of Schreber's behavior in the County Asylum at Sonnenstein (1894–1902), however, now reveal through an independent source that in that phase of his illness, Schreber appeared to have rather explicit castration and passive homosexual fears. . . .[2]

[2] E.g. "he imagined . . . his penis had been twisted off by an instrument which he called a 'nerve probe'; he maintained that he was a woman; but he also declared that he had to put up a strong resistance against the homosexual love of certain persons."

. . .

It would appear that the precipitating events in Schreber's illness must be viewed as events logically serving to instigate feelings of hostility, as well as homosexuality. That both kinds of impulses were fused in Schreber's delusion regarding Flechsig is not surprising in view of Mrs. Schreber's "worship" of the man whose picture, we are told, was kept on her desk for many years following Schreber's first attack of hypochondriasis. Mrs. Schreber's act of "gratitude" towards Flechsig would have offered constant reinforcement for Schreber's low self-esteem, facilitating the development of feelings of jealousy, competition, and rage. In this regard it is perhaps relevant to note that a major regression in Schreber's second illness apparently occurred during his wife's "holiday" and that his final hospitalization in 1907 followed immediately upon his wife's stroke.

. . .

I would like now to deal with some specific hypotheses which have been suggested through a review of a number of cases with paranoid symptomatology and to examine their relevance in relation to the Schreber data.

As one cuts through the variegated symptomatology—often rich in dramatic symbolic expressions which sometimes only lure and entice the investigator away from the basic issue—the immediately obvious and hence frequently overlooked phenomenon is related to the basic nature of a delusion, i.e., an unalterable conviction maintained about a disordered perception, which remains untouched and uncorrected by what is represented by others as reality and "common sense." In the words of the medical expert's report to the court on Schreber, "the patient is filled with pathological ideas . . . *not amenable to correction by objective evidence and judgment of circumstances as they really are*" (Macalpine and Hunter, 1955).

. . .

We can only speculate on the kind of perception or deception which may have played such a role in Schreber's disorder. Some clue as to the presence of an ongoing disturbance in communication, however, has been given by the important biographical data supplied by Niederland (1959, 1960). It now seems likely that one issue may have centered about the father's sanity. Niederland's suggestion that the case history reported by the senior Schreber (presumably of a chance acquaintance suffering from "attacks of melancholia, morbid brooding, and tormenting criminal impulses") may have been autobiographical, is, I believe, quite plausible. In any event, a system of therapeutic gymnastics which permitted the father to express sadistic impulses to his son while verbalizing a quite different morality, presented the son with diverse implications which the memoirs give no evidence of ever having been successfully resolved.

In connection with Schreber's castration fears, Dr. Niederland has recently called my attention to his newly uncovered data which indicate that castration was a procedure actually used in Flechsig's clinic for certain mental conditions. It is not unlikely that Schreber knew this.

Another inference presenting itself in a study of case histories is related to the presence of megalomaniacal trends inherent in any delusional system. Although Macalpine and Hunter (1956) conclude that megalomania is by no means an invariable concomitant of delusions of persecution, case histories would appear to support the contention that implicit in all delusions is the assumption that the persecuted is a very important person to be the central figure in the drama arising from his own projections. As indicated by Schreber, ". . . everything that happens is in reference to me. . . ."

. . .

One final word in relation to the role of paternal and maternal influences in the genesis of paranoid dynamics. The degree of pathogenic influence of either parent differs significantly from case to case in the variations which arise in those disorders which encompass problems around sexual identification. The results of the previously reported study on identical twins with diverse overt psychopathology (Rainer *et al.*, 1960) appear consistent with the recent statement of Cooley (1959) which places emphasis on the part of both parental figures in responding differentially to the child in terms of sexual identity. While the parent of the same sex is usually assumed to be the model for appropriate sexual identification, the role of the opposite-sex parent, as the model of what one's own sex is not, is sometimes as important. The cruel fate dealt Schreber included among other things, it would seem, models who confused rather than delineated aspects of their son's identity as a man, and ultimately as a human being.

19 / A Note on Soul Murder: Vampire Fantasies

Merl M. Jackel

Students of Schreber's *Memoirs* from Freud to the present have been fascinated by the questions of the origin and possible meanings of what Schreber, in typical paranoid fashion, alludes to as "soul murder." Freud's statements on this issue are unclear. He quotes Schreber: "[The object of the conspiracy against me was that] I should be handed over to a certain person in such a manner that my soul should be delivered up to him, but my body . . . should be transformed into a female body, and as such surrendered to the person in question with a view to sexual abuse. . . ." Yet, Freud does not regard this as being equated with soul murder. Rather he follows in frustration Schreber's allusions to Goethe's *Faust* and Byron's *Manfred*, ending with the comment that "the essence and secret of the latter work is brother-sister incest" (Freud, 1911, p. 44). Curiously, Freud omits the passage immediately preceding the literary references, in which Schreber discusses the concept of soul murder, which I quote:

To start with . . . the idea is widespread in the folk-lore and poetry of all peoples that it is somehow possible to take possession of another person's soul in order to prolong one's life at another soul's expense, or to secure some other advantages which outlast death. One has only to think for example of Goethe's *Faust*, Lord Byron's *Manfred*, Weber's *Freischütz*, etc. Commonly, however, the main role is supposed to be played by the Devil, who entices a human being into selling his soul to him by means of a drop of blood, etc. for some worldly advantages. (MacAlpine and Hunter, 1955, p. 55)

The content of this passage made me suspect that Schreber harbored somewhere a Vampire fantasy not rarely found in analytic patients who suffered from impotence fixated on or regressed to an anal-sadistic level. The *Encyclopedia Britannica* defines "vampire" as "Blood-sucking ghosts. Original meaning is supposed to be the soul of a dead man which quits the dead body at night to suck the blood of living persons. Hence, when the grave is opened, the corpse is found to be fresh. To put a stop to his ravages the commonest method is to drive a stake through the body."

The congruence is striking. Yet I could find no conclusive confirmation in the *Memoirs*. I was, therefore, delighted to find in Baumeyer's report specific confirmation; he quotes from the old hospital records concerning Schreber: "The contents of the delusions obviously changed frequently, but in the last phase of his stay in the Leipzig Clinic he believed that he would be tortured to death in a terrible way. He lost himself more and more in mystical religious fantasies; God spoke to him and *vampires* and demons made game of him" (italics added).

Jones has written extensively on Vampire fantasies from the psychoanalytic, anthropological and mythological aspects. Much of what he says is applicable to Schreber. I quote only a few pertinent excerpts. He emphasizes that the vampire is a "revenant," derived from the "incest complex" with its attendant love, hate, and guilt. "The vampire fantasy implies a continued interest of the living in the dead," which may be unconsciously desired, feared, and/or projected. (Schreber's relationship with his father comes to mind; Niederland, 1960). "A further complexity is introduced by the beliefs in which the vampire-like spirit emanates not from a dead but from a living person." This suggests aspects of Schreber's relationship to Flechsig.

In general it may be said that the habit of sucking living blood is throughout connected with ideas of cannibalism on the one hand and the Incubat-Succubat, two facts which alone reveal the sexual origin of the belief (Jones).

The explanation of these fantasies is surely not hard to find. A nightly visit from a beautiful or frightful being, who first exhausts the sleeper with passionate embraces and then withdraws from him a vital fluid: all this can point only to a natural and common process, namely to nocturnal emissions accompanied with dreams of a more or less erotic nature. In the unconscious mind blood is commonly an equivalent for semen . . . (Jones).

Turning now to Schreber's *Memoirs,* we know that in February, 1894, three months after his hospitalization, Schreber's wife left for a four-day visit to her father. At this point his illness took a turn for the worse. Schreber writes, "Decisive for my mental collapse was one particular night; during that night I had a quite unusual number of pollutions (perhaps half a dozen)." Can we not assume that in her absence Schreber was flooded by increased homosexual longings for his doctor? It was following these events that he developed the delusion that his wife was dead.

I believe that by "soul-murder," Schreber meant submission to the male (Flechsig) at various levels of libidinal development. At the oral level, it meant to be eaten, sucked dry; at the anal level, to be drained and humiliated; at the phallic level, to be castrated, made into a woman. Elements from the oral and anal levels are represented in Vampire fantasies which at times became manifest in Schreber's delusions.

Bibliography for Part III

Chapter 16

1. Erikson, E. *Childhood and Society.* (New York: Norton, 1950.)
2. Federn, P. *Ego Psychology and the Psychoses.* (New York: Basic Books, 1952.)
3. Ferenczi S. (1923). *Thalassa, A Theory of Genitality.* (Albany: Psychoanalytic Quarterly, 1938.)
4. Loewald, H. (1951). "Ego and Reality." *Int. J. Psycho-Anal.,* 32:10–18.
5. Macalpine, I. and Hunter, R. *Daniel Paul Schreber. Memoirs of My Nervous Illness.* (London: Dawson, 1955.)
6. Niederland, W. (1951). "Three Notes on the Schreber Case." *Psychoanal. Quart.* 20:579–591.

Chapter 17

Baumeyer, F. (1956). "The Schreber Case." *Int. J. Psycho-Anal.,* 37:61–74.
Erikson, E. H. (1950). *Childhood and Society.* (New York: Norton.)
——— (1959). "Identity and the Life Cycle." *Psychological Issues,* 1:1–171.
Freud, S. (1911). "Psycho-Analytic Notes upon an Autobiographical Account of a Case of Paranoia (Dementia Paranoides)." *S.E.* 12.
Macalpine, I., and Hunter, R. (1955). *Daniel Paul Schreber. Memoirs of My Nervous Illness.* (London: Dawson.)
——— ——— (1956). *Schizophrenia, 1677.* (London: Dawson.)
Niederland, W. (1951). "Three Notes on the Schreber Case." *Psychoanal. Quart.,* 20:579–591.
——— (1959a). "Schreber: Father and Son." *Psychoanal. Quart.,* 28:151–169.
——— (1959b). "The 'Miracled-Up' World of Schreber's Childhood," *Psychoanal. Study Child,* 14:383–413.
——— (1960). "Schreber's Father." *J. Amer. Psychoanal. Assoc.,* 8:492–499.
Schreber, D. (1865). *Das Buch der Erziehung an Leib und Seele.* (Leipzig: Fleischer, 3rd ed., 1891.)
White, R. B. (1961). "The Mother-Conflict in Schreber's Psychosis." *Int. J. Psycho-Anal.,* 42:55–73.

Chapter 18

Baumeyer, F. (1956). "The Schreber Case." *Int. J. Psycho-Anal.*, 37:61–74.

Cooley, T. (1959). "The Nature and Origins of Psychological Sexual Identity." *Psychol. Rev.*, 66:165–177.

Freud, S. (1911). "Psycho-Analytic Notes upon an Autobiographical Account of a Case of Paranoia (Dementia Paranoides)." *S.E.*, 12.

Friedmann, M. (1908). "Contributions to the Study of Paranoia." *Nerv. Ment. Dis. Monogr.*, 2.

Gierlich, N. (1908). "Periodic Paranoia and the Origin of Paranoid Delusions." *Nerv. Ment. Dis. Monogr.*, 2.

Glick, B. S. (1959). "Homosexual Panic, Clinical and Theoretical Considerations." *J. Nerv. Ment. Dis.*, 129:20–28.

Klein, H. & Horwitz, W. A. (1949). "Psychosexual Factors in the Paranoid Phenomena." *Amer. J. Psychiat.*, 105:697–701.

Macalpine, I., and Hunter, R. (1955). *Daniel Paul Schreber. Memoirs of My Nervous Illness.* (London: Dawson.)

——— ——— (1956). *Schizophrenia, 1677.* (London: Dawson.)

Niederland, W. (1959). "The 'Miracled-Up' World of Schreber's Childhood." *Psychoanal. Study Child*, 14.

——— (1960). "Schreber's Father." *J. Amer. Psychoanal. Assn.*, 8:492–499.

Rainer, J. D., Mesnikoff, A., Kolb, L. C., and Carr, A. (1960). "Homosexuality and Heterosexuality in Identical Twins." *Psychosom. Med.*, 22:251–259.

Searles, M. F. (1961). "The Sources of Anxiety in Paranoid Schizophrenia." *Brit. J. Med. Psychol.*, 34:129–141.

Waelder, R. (1951). "The Structure of Paranoid Ideas." *Int. J. Psycho-Anal.*, 32:167–177.

White, R. B. (1961). "The Mother-Conflict in Schreber's Psychosis." *Int. J. Psycho-Anal.*, 42:55–73.

Chapter 19

Baumeyer, F. (1956), "The Schreber Case," *Int. J. Psycho-Anal.*, 37:61–74.

Freud, S. (1911), "Psycho-Analytic Notes upon an Autobiographical Account of a Case of Paranoia (Dementia Paranoides)." *Standard Ed.*, 12:9–82.

Jones, E. (1949), *On the Nightmare.* London: Hogarth Press.

Macalpine, I., and Hunter, R. A. (1955), *Memoirs of My Nervous Illness.* London: Dawson.

Niederland, W. (1960), "Schreber's Father," *J. Amer. Psychoanal. Assn.*, 8:492–499.

Index